The Battle for Kingdom Identity

Our Spiritual Authority

The Battle for Kingdom Identity

Our Spiritual Authority

Rev. Velma D. White

THE BATTLE FOR KINGDOM IDENTITY

Copyright © 2015 by Rev. Velma D White

Published by Rev. Velma D White

Edited by Lori Byers, Dorothy Carbert

All rights reserved. Neither this publication or any part of this publication may be reproduced or transmitted in any form or by any means, electronic or mechanical, including photocopying, recording or any information storage and retrieval system, without the written permission from the author.

The author can be contacted via email: *velforjesus@gmail.com*, or P.O. Box 10 Ft. Providence, NT X0E 0L0

ISBN: 978-1-927588-92-5

Unless otherwise identified, all Scriptures are taken from the King James/Amplified Parallel Edition Grand Rapids, Michigan 4930, U.S.A. Published by Zondervan, Zondervan Corporation Copyright © 1995. Scripture quotations taken from the Amplified Bible, Copyright © 1954, 1958, 1962, 1964, 1965, 1987 by Lockman Foundation. All rights reserved. Used by permission (www.Lockman.org)

Scripture quotations taken from the New King James Version. Copyright © 1979, 1980, 1982 by Thomas Nelson, Inc. Used by Permission. All rights reserved.

Scripture quotations take from The Living Bible, Copyright © 1992 by Tyndale House Publishers, Inc, Wheaton, Il 60189. All rights reserved.

Scripture quotations marked HCSB have been take from the Holman Christian Standard Bible®, Copyright © 1999, 2000, 2002, 2003, 2009 by Holman Bible Publishers. Used by Permission. Holman Christian Standard Bible®, Holman CSB®, and HCSB® are federally trademarks of Holman Bible Publishers

Scripture is taken from God's Word®. © 1995 God's Word to the Nations. Used by permission of Baker Publishing Group.

Scripture quotations marked NLT are taken from Holy Bible, New Living Translation, copyright © 1996, 2004, 2007 by Tyndale House Foundation. Used by permission of Tyndale House Publishers, Inc., Carol Stream, Illinois 60188. All rights reserved.

Scripture quotations taken from CEV, Contemporary English Version, copyright © 1995, American Bible Society

Scripture taken from the HOLY BIBLE, NEW LIFE VERSION, Copyright © 1969, 1976, 1978, 1986, 1992, 1997, Christian Literature International, P. O. Box 777, Canby, Or 97013. Used by Permission.

Publication assistance and
digital printing in Canada by

www.pagemaster.ca

Foreword:

Rev. Velma White's latest book, *The Battle for Kingdom Identity*, is an important follow-up to her first book, *Redeeming Culture* in which she challenged her readers to recognize that the cross of Christ cuts across every culture. Her second book is a call for followers of Jesus to see the necessity of allegiance to God's Kingdom. For the past 45 years, my involvement in urban and rural communities across North America as well as in Eastern Europe, Africa, Asia and the Caribbean has given me opportunity to see the challenges for those in every culture to truly "see and enter" the Kingdom of God. (*John 3:3 and 5*) Velma's ministry and experience across many communities in northern Canada has prepared her well in addressing principles of identity that are far-reaching and apply to every culture. Many Christians do not seem to grasp the full scope of the fact that God's Kingdom has its own culture. The author describes, in a clear and simple manner, the Kingdom of God as a melting pot that is made up of those from every culture who have discovered their primary identity to be as true followers of Jesus Christ.

The Battle for Kingdom Identity addresses an important clarification of the Kingdom of God. Some, who read the scriptures, mistakenly assume that the phrases "kingdom of God" or "kingdom of Heaven" refers solely to the place of a Christian's destiny after death. While heaven is real and certainly is in God's domain, His kingdom includes much more than our final destination. God's kingdom also includes His rule and reign in the lives of His people, the church on earth. Thank God for hope for an eternal home in heaven! However, if hope for the future is our only goal, then it is no wonder that the church is often narrowly focussed on salvation of the individual as an end rather than understanding that we are "saved" and called for a much larger purpose. While we live *in* this world, Jesus makes it very clear that His followers are not "*of* this world". In Christ, we find a new identity! Velma White has grasped the understanding that God's kingdom does not erase our racial or cultural identity but a willing acceptance of our new identity in God's Kingdom lifts us into a broader way of thinking and living. In Chapter 8, she presents insight into the need to separate from those parts of our natural culture that are not in harmony with God's Kingdom. Each of Jesus' followers are "born from above" to grow in grace coming to full maturity and identity in the body of Christ leaving behind those cultural ways that are not harmonious with God's kingdom ways. As mature members we can work together in God's kingdom offering hope to a broken world both for this life and the life to come.

This book will serve the church well in helping to address some of the issues related to the conflicts that often occur when we try to define and decide between allegiances to our birth culture versus our "new birth" culture. We are urged by the author to look at our birth culture through the scrutiny of God's eyes to determine what we can retain and what must be discarded. Whether you are a new Christian or one seasoned with years of faith in Christ, you will be challenged to accept your identity in God's kingdom and the responsibility and authority to serve as His loyal Ambassador. Read this book and be instructed and blessed

Wayne Shenk,
Missions Consultant,
Vanderhoof, B. C.

Endorsements:

"Velma's book is a must read! I felt like she was talking about me at times. It is for anyone struggling with their identity in Christ. As a First Nations woman, some of the issue's she addressed in this book hit home. I know of others who would benefit a great deal from reading this book. I thank God for this book and the author. Very insightful."

Pastor Marcy Rosling,
Kawacatoose Lighthouse Ministries.
Kawacatoose, SK

"I have known Velma for many years. She is a Woman of God with integrity. I have seen her wrestle with her identity as a native woman and as a Christian. What she writes comes from hard experience and spiritual struggle. She presents a strong scriptural argument that will help you find that best of all identities, seeing yourself as a New Creation in Jesus Christ and a Child of the Heavenly Father. Reading this book could change your life!"

Pastor Larry Keegstra,
Camp Living Water Ministries
Vanderhoof, B.C.

"Journeys on unfamiliar terrain take courage and determination. To find personal identity or roots in the midst of the dynamics of quickly changing culture is one such journey, yet, in the uncertainty of these times many are endeavouring to do so. Velma D. White tackles this quest openly and honestly as she shares her journey of discovery as a first Nations believer in Christ. What she finds through diligently searching the Word of God may surprise you. Share her journey as she finds the way that scripturally transcends the protocols of culture, finding not only her roots, identity and purpose but also the peace and joy that belongs to citizens of the Kingdom. Well done Velma — a book well worth reading."

Rev. M. L. (Lori) Byers,
New Testament Outreach Ministries Int.
Ft. Providence, NT

"Who are we?

Where did we come from?

Why are we here?

Does it even matter?

Who do we belong to?

What do we do with our past?

Can we rise above our past or does our past determine our future?

What is our purpose in life?

What does it mean to be a part of the Kingdom of God?

These are important questions about our identity and the Kingdom of God. These are some of the questions that Velma addresses and answers through Scripture as well as sharing examples from life experience.

The challenge is laid out before us to lay hold of the truths of the Kingdom of God. Often there is a battle to realize that our true identity as believers is found in Jesus and we are part of His Kingdom and all other kingdoms will bow before Him.

Good work Velma and thanks for the challenge you have put before us all."

Rev. Dorothy Carbert,
New Testament Outreach Ministries Int.
Ft. Providence, NT

THIS BOOK IS DEDICATED TO:

All those who have laid down their lives in order for us to have the truth of the Gospel imparted into our hearts, which in turn, causes us to do the same. Thank you for your dedication and service in the higher call of God in Christ Jesus!

IN LOVING MEMORY OF:

Glenna Cumming
1962-2014

THANK YOU:

To Jesus my Lord and Saviour, the Love of my life – thank you for dying for my sins and redeeming my life with your loving kindness!

To my wonderful father for blessing me on my life's journey.

To my wonderful mother for never giving up on me and pointing me to the One who is The Way, The Truth and The Life - Jesus.

To Pastor Lori Byers and Pastor Dorothy Carbert for always believing in me, for your Christ like example in the work of the Gospel, for your love and friendship as well as leadership in my life. It is such a privilege to work together with you in the Harvest Field of the Vineyard. Thank you for your input.

To all the NTOMI ministry team for your encouragement and dedication in the work of the ministry in every area.

To Camp Living Water Ministries and all their various ministry teams who so faithfully and for so many long years have reached out to our native children and youth imparting the hope of knowing Jesus into the hearts of these forgotten ones.

To Pastor Larry Keegstra, Pastor Wayne Shenk and Pastor Marcy Rosling – thank you for your input.

Table of Contents

The Cross of Healing and Forgiveness 1

Introduction 19

Three Common Factors 24

God Wants To Communicate With Man 28

In The Beginning 32

God Sees It All 40

Life Is Not About Us 48

Christianity And Religion 53

There Is A "Cult" In Culture 59

Spiritual Authority Is Two-Fold: Part One 74

Spiritual Authority Is Two-Fold: Part Two 86

Spiritual Authority Is Progressive 91

Our Motivation 99

Conclusion 108

End Notes 110

PROLOGUE

The Cross of Healing and Forgiveness

LOVE BROKE THROUGH

It seems that what we face in this life – this space of time to which we are allotted can either make us or break us. In either case, we are shaped. *"I am a product of my past,"* is what I once believed. If this is true, then how can I look forward to the future with anticipation of something better? How then, could I face the future when all I saw in my past were the marred images of family dysfunction, betrayed trust and a God who has been sadly misrepresented?

At eight years old, I sometimes desired to die and end my life because I could not see the future as being different from my current life experience. I would wish I was only in a bad dream and one day I would wake up and life would no longer be a miserable experience. It goes without saying that, yes, I do have fond and happy memories in my childhood. The bad experiences I have had, seemed to have blocked out those good experiences.

It has taken an inner healing process by the power of God's grace to remember those good times. I am thankful for this.

I was introduced to the Gospel of Jesus Christ at a Bible camp for Native children. It was one of my most treasured places to be as a child. There is where I know that I felt safe, I felt the presence of God and those that worked at this camp, were very kind and loving people.

Throughout much of my childhood, I went through abuse; physical, sexual, and spiritual. I was physically abused by my teachers in elementary school. I recall a particular teacher who, in her frustration, would scream in my ears, pull my hair causing my nose to bleed, and call me *"stupid Indian!"*. Those into whose care I was entrusted while my parents were away, had abused me sexually. I did not realize that what I was facing as a child was sexual abuse. I thought it was normal. But no one knew, and for fear of my abusers, I remained silent and ashamed. I had a way of keeping things well hidden.

To make things worse, it was under the guise of religion at a religious institution that I experienced on going spiritual abuse. It was through this experience, that my heart became hard and I turned against God. At 12 years old, I began to dabble with satanic worship and was heavily influenced through the secular heavy metal music I listened to. I also began to believe Satan's lies and was lured to the path of destruction.

At age 13, our family moved to where my parents could attend Bible School for a season. The people I met there reminded me so much of the people I met at camp. They were kind and loving Christians. By this time in my life, I was no longer soft to the Lord. My heart had become bitter. I was untrusting of all Christians and purposely misbehaved in church and at youth meetings.

I began to self-destruct emotionally and hated myself for the things that my abusers did to me as a child. It began to torment me day and night. I could not concentrate in school. I was tormented with thoughts of suicide. I scratched and cut myself because of the pain deep within. The evil spirits that tormented me told me that it was too late to go back to God. Through all this, God used these loving Christian people, to patiently reach out to me in spite of my refusal to accept Jesus back into my life.

After a year of this inner torment because of my painful childhood memories, self-hatred and condemnation, God broke though the cloud of darkness which held me in deep bondage. That breakthrough took place at a Family Camp Meeting that was held at a Bible School where I witnessed many people in the audience receive a miracle of healing in their bodies. I could sense the presence of God in this meeting - and everywhere in the building and on the property. The evil spirits that tormented me, no matter how loud their voices were, could not stop the voice of God.

Deep in my heart I wanted to come back to God, but I did not know if He would want me back. It was during this meeting where I heard so softly, and yet so strongly,

Jesus calling my name. Interestingly, I recognized His voice. Although I was backslidden, I still knew His voice. Right there in the back row of that church service, Jesus called my name and He told me that He loved me and wanted me to come home to Him.

I chose to listen to His voice and yielded my heart and life to Him right at that moment. His love was so strong that I knew that He had forgiven me for turning away from Him. I asked Him to fill me with His Holy Spirit and I began to experience His deep touch. All the darkness that tormented me fled away. The next day, I gathered all my occult items and secular heavy metal music and destroyed them and threw them into the garbage. I was changed! Jesus came into my heart anew. Those around me began to see the evidence of it in the weeks and months to follow.

Our family moved back to our reserve and I regret to say that I was not faithful to the Lord through my high school years. At age 16, I ran into some trouble with some friends and became desperate to get away from my community for a little while. My mother thought it best that I take the bus to camp and volunteer for the month in hopes that I would come through to God. My walk with God was unstable as far as living a life that pleased Him as a young person, but I would not harden my heart towards the Lord, no matter what we faced as a family or how discouraged I felt. I would not turn back to the occult.

However, I did not turn to the Lord for comfort or strength. Instead, I turned to drugs and alcohol to help me feel happy. Of course, these did not remedy how I felt deep within. Most of my friends would party because of being bored with life, I did not go to parties because of boredom of life but because it just seemed like a quick way to get rid of the inner sadness I felt.

In 1993, I left my home reservation and went to stay with Christian friends in Red Deer. I volunteered at the Bible Camp for the month of July. At the age of 18, I felt like such a failure at serving God. I knew I needed to make things right with God, especially if I was going to work at this Bible Camp. My friend invited me to come to a tent meeting in town and had already arranged a ride for the both us. As we waited for our ride to show up, I went to the back alley to have a smoke and I heard God calling me again, He said, *"Do not put me out like a cigarette, choose this day whom you will serve"*. I admitted to God that I didn't know how to be a Christian and I was a failure and then pleaded for His help to live a life that pleased Him. We went to the meeting and that night at the end of the service, I walked over to the altar to rededicate my life to Jesus. I have not turned back since. Glory to God!

THE HEALING BEGINS

A week later, a Christian lady whom I had been visiting felt led by the Holy Spirit to pray for me and shared with me that I needed to learn what it was to trust and that Jesus would show me who I could trust. She apologized on behalf of the things done to our people by white people from past generations. I did not understand what she meant.

That night the Holy Spirit began to minister to me and I believe it was at that point that God began to crack open the hard shell I had formed around my heart – my inability to feel anything. As I began to sense His Spirit touching my heart, I cried out loud as a deep groan of emotional pain was released from within me. I did not understand then but I realize now that God was after my heart and He had begun a deep inner cleansing and healing.

Four years later, I had completed two years of Bible School and had already begun to serve as an interim pastor for a small Native fellowship. At that time, a yearly conference was held at the organization I was working with. The topic at the conference: "repentance and reconciliation". The target group was the spiritual fathers and generation "X". I was included in the generation "X" age group at that time. They called our age group to the stage and the spiritual fathers (those in ministry and leadership) were also called to the stage – those who felt led to participate. These pastors began to repent to our age group for the hurt they caused our generation in that God had been misrepresented to our generation through them as our spiritual fathers.

Though I was not expecting this kind of repentance to be addressed publicly, it was at that moment that the deep pain in my heart surfaced. The painful memories of the spiritual abuse I experienced as a child at the religious institution I had attended flooded my heart and mind. I collapsed to floor of the stage and wept bitterly. One of the pastors who was also on the stage held my hand and wept with me. All I could do was weep. I was unable to hold back my emotional composure. God has truly had His hand upon me and knows how much we can handle when it is time to face those difficult things that we need to face. Truly, He is our Healer.

THE CROSS OF FORGIVENESS

Since then I have been learning what it means to forgive those teachers. At odd times throughout my life, certain incidences trigger memories from that school. Every time emotional pain would surface, I would talk to my pastors with whom I am in ministry today and they would pray with me. I wondered if these bad memories would ever go away. Perhaps this next prayer will finish the healing process. I finally came to realize how much I needed to deal with this painful memory.

It wasn't until we had returned to my home reservation a third time to hold a series of tent meetings that I realized how deep that pain had been. Two weeks prior to our return the Lord forewarned me that four specific people would be attending the meetings. He gave me assurance that He would walk me through it as I faced them. To tell you the truth, I was nervous about it. It was this cross that I had feared. I kept reminding myself of Jesus' words, we are to forgive others or we will not be forgiven. Jesus Himself prayed for those who crucified Him and asked God to forgive them too. I had to prove that I had truly forgiven, and proving it was to face them.

Two years earlier, I was able to face the care-givers who had abused me when I was a child. I was genuinely happy to see them getting touched by the Lord in the tent meetings we held two years prior in one of my auntie's yard. I began to realize that if I could face those caregivers and show them forgiveness, then I could do so with these teachers and leaders from the religious institution.

During each and every tent meeting we hold we make prayer meetings a priority. As our team gathered to pray for the meetings and for the community on the first day of this particular set of meetings, I confessed to our Gospel tent ministry team the struggle and the war within me. They gathered around me and prayed for healing so that I would be released from my ties to the past. I knew what I had to do next.

After the prayer meeting, I drove to that old school building. It still remained standing but it was very run down. The grass was almost three feet high. I walked around the school and looked inside the windows and began to pray and sever myself spiritually from the painful memory of this school. I anointed myself and the ground with oil and thanked Jesus for setting me free. I then drove to where the school now was being held, and I anointed the ground with oil and asked God for a revival in at that school.

I did not think that these people, whom the Lord showed me would be there, would actually attend the tent meetings. Perhaps, I thought, God was just wanting to check my heart and let me deal with it anyway. But lo and behold, the second last night, they showed up. I knew that they probably forgot what had happened those years ago and the thought came to me, "Although they were well intended, at that time, these people were caught up in a religious spirit and were convinced they were led by the Lord to do what they did to me."

Often times, religious spirits are expressed through legalism and the abusive use of spiritual authority. Although my past experience of this had left deep scars, God had healed me and done a work in my heart of forgiveness and I felt sorry for them, because they were used by the enemy. So as I sat on the stage with the rest of the musicians, I began to pray for them to be released of the effects of the past and that they could be all that they were meant to be in God and not miss the mark at the end of their lives.

To make matters more intense, I was to preach that night. My subject? The Lord had me to share of Gilgal, where the children of Israel were required of the Lord to become circumcised before they could take Jericho and enter the promise land. This generation had not been circumcised by their parents in the wilderness when Moses was leading them. The sign of their covenant with God was that every male had to be circumcised at eight days old. Their parents did not do this for them while they journeyed through the wilderness. Therefore the Lord required that they go through this procedure before they could take their promised land. In fact, their parents were no longer there indicating that they had to deal with this without them being present. However, this is what the Lord said after the moment of their compliance with Him on that day, *"This day I have rolled way the reproach of Egypt from among you"* – the reproach of their historical past (see Joshua 5).

That night I shared with all my heart the very Word that the Lord had given me to share. Sitting in the audience were the very perpetrators of the abuse. Right then and there I knew the Lord had so worked in my heart such forgiveness and freedom, that I prayed earnestly for them to also experience the reproach of their past being rolled away and that they would walk in the freedom that only Jesus can give. I did not get the chance to shake hands with each one who had been involved because some had left during the altar call. But when the time of ministering at the altar was over, I went to the others to greet them.

As I made my way over, I could see that one of them was nervous. When I reached her, I grabbed her hand and then embraced her. Without saying a word, she was no longer tense but relaxed and I knew that she knew she was forgiven. I silently prayed over her to be set free from the reproach of the past and that she could be all that God had called her to be.

I collapsed in my bed that night as I was exhausted from the emotional ups and downs of the week thus far. Yet, this time the pain deep within was truly gone and I felt so free and grateful. The cross that I had feared was now a memorial of what the Lord had done. I look back now and I am amazed at the incredible grace of God and how truly nothing is too hard or too complicated for God to heal. When we simply choose to yield to His grace and take the bold step to forgive to the uttermost, it is amazing what He will do. Forgiveness is powerful! It is there at the Cross of Jesus that we are truly set free and can come to true resolve and healing. Those seemingly unforgiveable things are not so seemingly unforgiveable. It is completely possible to do so but only by the love, mercy and grace of the Lord. He has forgiven me of all my sins, therefore I make the choice walk out that forgiveness and freely forgive.

A REVELATION UNFOLDED

A revelation unfolded that night that as I began to realize that the *unforgiveness* I held, made me susceptible to the false doctrine of syncretism (mixing of Native religion and Christian practices/worship). In my first book, *Redeeming Culture - The Other Side Of The Coin*, I addressed the issue of syncretism that has been lurking in many churches and Christian organizations today. I knew that God had called me to write this book. I shared how at one time I was involved with syncretism to some measure. I had used native culture - more specifically, I had used the sacred drum, dance and regalia as a means to express my worship to the Creator Jesus. It was during this phase in my life and ministry that I was challenged to search the Word and know what it says, I began to sincerely seek the Lord. Was what I was doing acceptable to God and was it agreeable with His Word?

I sincerely searched the scriptures and made a conscious choice to put aside my opinions as well as the viewpoints that others held on the matter regarding whether they were for it or against it. I recall asking God to speak to me and open my understanding to the truth of His Word. This began to happen as I meticulously studied the scriptures and came to find how wrong I was.

After completing my thesis, I took my native regalia to a friends place and, with my fellow-workers in the ministry, we built a fire in their back yard and I threw into the fire all the items I used to dance with in the church. It was in the middle of a spring evening when an unusual thing occurred. It was very dark at 8:30 p.m. and we could hear an eerie sound of birds above us flying away. However, there were no birds. We were hearing things in the spirit. I began to rejoice that it was the truth that had set me free! I knew I had to speak out on this subject wherever the Lord opened the door for me.

I also realized that what I had experienced at the religious institution where I attended as a child had caused me to feel justified in taking up the practice of the native drum and dance and "redeem" it for Christ. I felt that I was reclaiming my identity as a First Nations person, yet I did not want to practice native religion which is very much engrossed in witchcraft procedures. At that time I thought that perhaps if I left out the ceremonies of sweet-grass, sage, and sweat-lodges and simply used the sacred drum to sing songs to Jesus, it would be acceptable. In this I felt as though I was redeeming who I was as a First Nations person and that through this, my identity was being restored.

Several Christians, not familiar with native religion, had encouraged me to redeem my culture for Christ. Their hearts were for me but they did not understand the dark side of native religion. They simply were empathetic and did not want to make the same mistake that the residential schools had done in the past. I believe this empathy has been an open door to the deception of syncretism in many of the churches today. It has been a door of guilt. Guilt will often get you to compromise the Word of God in order to appease the offended party. It causes you to see unclearly and to lose your confidence in what God's Word says.

The open door for my native people has been through holding on to unforgiveness as well the need to feel justified and heard. This can only be resolved at the foot of the cross no matter how many apologies come our way. A case in point, recently a respected native elder had been publicly humiliated by security guards in a mall where he had been misjudged as an associate of some trouble makers who had been causing trouble in that same mall. These trouble-makers were banned from the mall. As he was having lunch in the food court, he was escorted out of the mall by several of the security personnel. This poor fellow was upset and embarrassed by this and went to the press with it.

A week later, the owner of that mall and several others who were in charge at that mall called this man to invite him to an official public apology. He came. The newspaper showed the spokesperson on her knees and with tears apologizing to this man for the humiliation he experienced at their mall. He accepted the apology but stated that he would not forgive and at that time would like to give it at least six months before he would considering forgiving the security guards. At least this fellow was honest about how he felt, however, it is sad to hear him say that he still would not forgive.

The bottom line for us all is whether or not we will forgive from our heart or choose to continue to harbour resentment even after being apologized to. As believers it is important for us to understand that forgiveness is the way of Christianity. God still leaves us with the choice to forgive and if we chose not to forgive, we are the ones in who remain in pain.

Some have chosen to walk the path of forgiveness whether apologized to or not. However, unfortunately many of our native people still harbour unforgiveness in spite of having been to several public reconciliation events. Those who have been wronged have participated in sharing their tears of their past experiences from the residential schools and also have partaken in the hearing of official public apologies from leaders representing the groups who caused their harm.

It is to my amazement that many of them still continue to hate white people. Their hearts were unchanged. I recall a respected lady in one community who having been to one of these kinds of conferences, made it clear to me that she refuses to ever forgive the priests and nuns for what they did to her when she attended the residential school as a child. If only she knew the freedom of letting go and coming into true inner healing.

I have briefly shared my personal experience of abuse, in order for readers who have gone through similar things to know that they are not alone. After coming to realize how I became susceptible to syncretism, I also understand why other false teachings can easily sway others. Paul's desire for believers was, *"that we should no longer be children tossed to and fro and carried about with every wind of doctrine,..."* (Ephesians 4:14a, NKJV). Peter warns, *"But there were also false prophets among the people, even as there will be false teachers among you, who will bring in destructive heresies..."* (2 Peter 1:1a, NKJV). These false teachers prey on broken, hurting and gullible people; people who are not grounded in the truth of God's Word. The resentment I held towards the teachers at the religious institution which I attended, caused my heart to become a breeding ground for deception. However, God in His mercy had His hand upon me and kept me from going further down this path of deception. Since I have chosen to walk the path of forgiveness and be true to His Word doing a work in my heart, I have been able to understand the dynamics that opened the door in my life to this false doctrine of syncretism.

Jesus said, *"...If you abide in my Word, you are My disciples indeed. And you shall know the truth and the truth shall make you free"* (John 8:31b-32, NKJV). Abiding in His Word has become my life's ambition – to really know Him Who is the Truth. By abiding in His Word I have also come to truly understand my true identity in Christ. I have also come to understand what my spiritual authority is based on, and from there I can boldly proclaim the Gospel of Jesus Christ. To those who follow Jesus, His words speak loud and clear on a regular basis:

> *...If anyone desires to come after Me, let him deny himself, and take up his cross daily, and follow Me. For whoever desires to save his life will lose it, but whoever loses his life for My sake will save it. For what profit is it to a man if he gains the whole world, and is himself destroyed or lost? For whoever is ashamed of Me, and My words, of him the Son of Man will be ashamed when He comes in His own glory, and in His Father's and of the holy angels* (Luke 9:23-26, NKJV).

I invite you to continue with me as we explore from the Word of God the answers to the prevalent issues that we face today regarding our true identity – where it was lost, how it was restored, and also what it means to walk in true spiritual authority - based on who we are in Christ and our submission to Him.

CHAPTER ONE

Introduction

We need to know *who* we are *in Christ* and never be moved from this reality.

FIRST THINGS FIRST

Before you begin reading the rest of this book, I would like to do a little exercise with you, if you are willing to participate. Take time now to write on a piece of paper (or on the next page) about yourself. These are things I would like you to address:

- Where you were born and where you now reside
- About your faith and the language you speak
- What you like or dislike
- What do you love about life, what are your hobbies, etc.

Well, now that you have written on a piece of paper about yourself, do you realize it was about you? Well, you say, you asked to me write about myself. You are right. I did it simply because it is easier to write about ourselves than about another person. In most cases, we are more certain of ourselves than we are about others. We can only assume what we know of another person, even those closest to us. Yet, even so, they themselves could best write about themselves.

Why have we taken this little exercise to write about ourselves? To see that often, we spend much of our lives trying to discover who we are and what our significance in this life is about. Why were we born? Are we an accident? Why did God make us the way we look? Why did He give us the personality He gave us? What is our purpose in this life for anyway? For many people, these are important questions. The good news is: God has the answer.

Most often, we come into Christianity with a self-centered point of view. That is, until we are introduced to the concept that we are chosen of God and appointed to fulfill His purposes. This discovery still keeps us focused on ourselves until we begin to understand the heart of God as to why He chose us. As new believers coming into Christianity, we are to learn to make our lives about God. **We are not doing God a favour by giving our lives to Him**. We are the ones in need of mercy and forgiveness. Therefore, if we desire to truly come to know who we are in Christ and our God-given identity, it is important to come to know Christ personally and we do this as we come into an intimate personal relationship with Him.

We also need to realize that God made us as we are simply because He is a God of variety, and not so that we could live selfish lives without His personal interaction in our lives. He made us in our uniqueness so that we could enjoy our own individual relationship with Him. Even so, our relationship with Him must be based on His standards and not our own standards. Although we are uniquely made and designed by God we are also made in His image. That is why I began this introduction with the first statement:

WE NEED TO KNOW *WHO* WE ARE *IN CHRIST* AND NEVER BE MOVED FROM THIS REALITY.

Our God-given purpose and design is based on knowing who we are in Christ - our true identity. This is where our confidence rests. It is from this reality that we can impact the world we live in and fulfill our God-given destiny. We were born to live and be a part of the Kingdom of Heaven. There are crucial things we must grasp in order to enter that Kingdom. How do we become a part of the Kingdom of Heaven? Well, Jesus told Nicodemus that we must become born again. We must repent of our sins and receive Christ Jesus as our only personal Lord and Saviour. When we do so, we come under His rule and His authority. Something supernatural takes place within our hearts and as we receive Christ Jesus, we are born again spiritually. Without that first taking place none of us will ever have the right to enter the Kingdom of Heaven (see John 3:3).

Speaking of kingdom, is this the very thing that causes so much tension in the world? Upon observing history through to today, it is safe to conclude that mankind has sought to build a kingdom of its own in some form or another. Whether by wars, political promotion, economical advancement, established religions, business, or organizations and/or self-made images, humanity has sought to establish its own significance in this world. From the beginning of time, mankind has sought to answer the age old question of "Who am I and what am I here for?" Many have sought for answers through numerous and tireless explanations, however, God has intervened to answer that question for us through the person of His Son - Jesus Christ. Lets' continue to look at our original identity in the following section.

CHAPTER TWO
Three Common Factors

What is identity and why is it important to so many today?

When looking at identity in the natural sense, we often relate three common factors:
- the language we speak
- the country which we were born
- and our ethnic back ground

Often, these factors are the common denominators that indicate our individual identity. Yet still, there is more to it than just that. It is important to understand the struggle that mankind has had in search for their identity and role in life. To some, identity and its significance is as a treasured possession; once they feel they have found it, they will cling to it and never let go. To others, it is not as important or as valuable, therefore they live life, day to day, existing and content to have their daily bread, a roof to sleep under and however life "works out" for them is fine. Others simply exist until the underlying question of their heart surfaces, with great desire to know "Who and why am I here?"

Let's look at one of the three common factors regarding mankind's identity: language. Language identifies one's national back ground. For instance: within Canada, if one's native language was French it would be easy to understand that person's background was French. The way you might come to that conclusion is not just in their speaking of the French language, but also in the strong accent, that is often linked to the French speaker as they speak in English. Now, what part of Canada that French speaking person came from would not be known but we can presume that individual is French by ethnic distinction. On the same note, there are also numerous other languages within Canada alone - aside from French and English, and besides other languages spoken by immigrants that come to live in Canada.

There are many native languages spread throughout Canada among the aboriginal peoples of this nation. *"First Nations languages within what is now Canada are classified into twelve separate groups of approximately fifty languages. The language groupings are broken down into different languages and dialects. Historians understand how groups identify themselves and interpret their environment though language."* [1] We also realize that they are very different and distinct from each other as they live in various types of environments across Canada.

The following statement gives us an example of one of those twelve groups. *"The ancestors of Athapaskan speakers dispersed throughout the Sub-Arctic region, with groups splitting away and moving onto the Plains and Plateau regions. The languages of the Athapaskan language group are Chipewyan, Beaver, Dene, Dene Dhaa, Tsuu T'ina (Sarcee),*

Sekani, Kaska, Tutchone, Han, and Gwich'n. All of these languages have several similar traits, which supports the theory that the ancestors of these speakers migrated relatively recently, and as a group."[2]

My personal experience can confirm this as I have traveled throughout the north-western parts of Canada and into Alaska. I have come to discover the common way of expressing *"thank you"* in most Northern languages is *"Mahsih."* This is the exact saying that is used among much of the Northern languages previously mentioned. We have only looked at one speaking group that has 10 tribal languages. We also realize that among the remaining parts of the World that there are countless languages all over the earth.

My purpose in bringing our attention to language is to recognize that *language is a gift*. It is given of God. Often mankind thinks that it was they themselves who created their own language. Sadly, certain religious institutions have told indigenous groups that their native language was of the devil. What mankind needs to understand is that their native language originated from the One Who created them. Could it be that perhaps this is why it was so traumatic when other people groups tried to suppress native languages such as the residential school experiences for First Nations in Canada? To suppress another's language is synonymous with the suppression of the very soul of the individual whom God has created. Language comes from God. He is the creator of all languages as we will discuss further as we look into Genesis 11:1-9.

Language is a part of who God created us to be. Yet we must understand that language was created for one purpose and that purpose was for *communication*. Therefore we must realize that...
God wants to communicate with man.

CHAPTER THREE

God Wants To Communicate With Man

"Society has lost its way completely, but society doesn't determine moral standards." [3]

We have to understand that the world (mankind) has lost its true identity through the deceitfulness of sin. God, in His Word tell us of how it was long ago. We read in Acts 14:8-14, how that both Paul and Barnabas were about to have had a sacrifice made to them by the people of Lystra. It was during Paul's preaching that he, by the power of God, healed a crippled man when he saw that this man had faith. The rest of the crowd assumed they were gods sent to them and so the people aroused one another to sacrifice to them as if they were gods. But Paul and Barnabas were horrified at their response to this miracle. They would not take payment for the miracle that was done. Instead, they tore their clothes in front of the crowd and began to testify:

> *Men! What are you doing? We are merely human beings like yourselves! We have come to bring you the Good News that you are invited to turn from the*

worship of these foolish things and pray instead to the living God, who made heaven and earth and sea and everything in them. In bygone days He permitted the nations to go their own ways, but He never left Himself without a witness; there were always his reminders - the kind things He did such as sending you rain and good crops and giving you food and gladness (Acts 14:15-17, T.L.B.).

We need to realize that this group of people that Paul and Barnabas were ministering to were not Jewish, nor did they have any knowledge of Jesus. They were completely ignorant of the Gospel. God sent Paul and Barnabas to preach to them at Lystra and one man, a crippled man, had faith in the words Paul spoke. God healed that man. Paul and Barnabas refused to be lifted up among them because they both knew the power did not come from them but from God who demonstrated His power as a sign to them.

The reason for the miracle that was done among them was to reveal God's love and compassion to them and that they would have faith in His Son Jesus. Because this group of people did not have an accurate knowledge of the supernatural, Barnabas and Paul had to start from the beginning to introduce the message of the gospel. He specifically says, "In bygone days He permitted the nations to go their own ways, but He never left Himself without a witness" (Vs. 16-17a). Paul was making reference to the beginnings of man's history after the time of the flood. Let's go further in Acts with Paul where he was in Athens and gives further insight to where he was coming from in these words:

> ...For as I was walking, I saw your many altars, and of them had this inscription of it - 'To the Unknown God'. You have been worshipping Him without knowing who He is, and now I wish to tell you about Him. He made the world and everything in it, and since He is Lord of Heaven and earth, He doesn't live in man-made temples; and human hands can't minister to His needs - for He has no needs! He himself give every need there is. He created all the people of the world and from one man, Adam, and scattered the nations across the face of the earth. He decided before hand which should rise and fall and when. He determined their boundaries. His purpose in all of this is that they should seek after God, and perhaps feel their way toward Him and find Him (so that they should seek the Lord in hope that they might grope for Him and find Him - NKJV) though He is not far from any one of us (Acts 17:23-27, T.L.B.),
>
> For in Him we live and move and our being, as also some of your own poets have said, 'for we are His offspring'. Therefore since we are the offspring of God, we ought not to think that the Divine Nature is like gold or silver or stone, something shaped by art of man's devising. Truly these times of ignorance God overlooked, but now commands all men everywhere to repent, because He has appointed a day on which

He will judge the world in righteousness by the Man He has ordained. He has given assurance of this to all by raising Him from the dead (Acts 17:28-31, NKJV).

Let's take time to clue in to what Paul was saying. Paul explains that the Lord created all people of the world from one man and then He scattered mankind across the face of the earth. He then gives *the purpose of why they were scattered* and that purpose was in order that mankind would *seek the Lord*. In this part of Acts, Paul was giving reference to both the time of creation and the time of the when the tower of Babel was built. In the earlier account from Acts 14 he states that God allowed them to go their own ways and He goes on to say in Acts 17 that in these times of ignorance God overlooked, but now He expects all men everywhere to repent and believe the Gospel of His Son. When we consider these words of Paul, we catch a glimpse of the dynamics regarding mankind's history in light of God's viewpoint. Since it was God who scattered the nations across the earth, why did He allow them to go their own ways? What were the times of ignorance? Why does He now expect all men everywhere to repent? To answer those questions, let us now turn to the book of beginnings...

CHAPTER FOUR

In The Beginning...

And the whole earth was of one language and of one speech. It came to pass, as they journeyed from the east, that they found a plain in the land of Shinar; and they dwelt there. And they said one to another, Go to, let us make brick, and burn them thoroughly. And they had brick for stone, and slime had they for mortar. and they said, go to , let us build a city and a tower, whose top may reach unto heaven; and let us make us a name, lest we be scattered abroad upon the face of the whole earth (Genesis 11:1-4, KJV).

From this passage of scripture we find that originally, the people on the earth knew they were of one identity - they also had one language. Mankind knew that his identity was *"that man was created in the image of God"*[4]. Romans 5 reveals how mankind became corrupt after the fall of man[5], as our very nature became corrupted by sin. Adam and Eve, our first ancestors, were acting on behalf of the human race. Their act of disobedience affected the whole human race forever (see Romans 5:12-14). Mankind was betrayed through Adam and turned over to Satan's kingdom which is the kingdom of darkness. The Kingdom of God was also betrayed.

Here we discover the loss of our true God-given identity and our right to have dominion (spiritual authority) in the way that God intended. Our world view of the fact that mankind was created in the image of God would be forever changed by man's first act of disobedience leading to the consequence of sin - death. John R. Cross relates a threefold dynamic which took place regarding man's relationship with God. First of all, death to man's relationship with God, secondly, death to the body by which we eventually will die and be separated from our body and thirdly, and finally death of judgement by which we would be eternally separated from God forever in the lake of fire.[6]

In spite of man's disobedience to God, God in His mercy promised a Deliverer that would deliver mankind from Satan's rule and would also crush Satan's head, the original seducer of Adam (see Genesis 3:15). From that time in man's history, man was taught by God to sacrifice a spotless lamb and offer its fat and blood on an altar to God. The blood sacrifice from that lamb would cover them and they would be made acceptable to God. However, prior to being shown this way, Adam and Eve attempted to make their own covering with fig leaves yet God did not accept it (see Genesis 3:8-21). Even after their attempt to make a covering for themselves they ran and hid from God when He came to visit them in the Garden of Eden. This behaviour reveals that they knew that their self-made covering was not enough to make them in right standing with God. Instead they felt shame, guilt and fear.

This is a picture of what we as humans do with our own sin. We often make excuses, we use our culture, traditions and religions to deal with our spiritual nakedness and we inherently know that it is not enough to make us acceptable to God. Today we claim that our First Nations people of North America had lost their identity through the assimilation of the residential school system. As detrimental as these things were to our people, do we realize that there are numerous ethnic groups across the earth that have gone through similar and even worse traumas than our own? As special as our case is, as First Nations people, and in light of what others have experienced in this world, only Jesus knows how to heal and restore the most broken and shattered heart. I make this statement for us to realize that we need to deal with the real heart issues of the matter.

I believe that we need to look further into mankind's history, and we need to go as far back to our first ancestors - Adam and Eve. It is there in Genesis, that we discover where and when the true loss of our identity took place. We will study further after the account of the tower of Babel, how that today the culture and religion which we have always known had become a counterfeit covering to the spiritual condition within us as humans from the time of Adam and Eve's fall.

After God dealt with their disobedience, Adam and Eve were shown how to come to God His way. In Genesis 3:21, God had made both Adam and Eve a covering; an innocent animal had to die, by the shedding of its' blood in order that they could be properly clothed. This was in place of their self-made covering. It was God who provided the solution to their nakedness. We discover in Genesis 4:1-5 how that a blood sacrifice was what God would accept and atonement was made for man. It was through this blood covering that mankind would maintain their relationship with God until the Promised Deliverer came to restore them back to their original creation and reconcile mankind back to God.

This short overview gives us the background of the dynamics/issues inherent in the account we read earlier regarding the tower of Babel from Genesis 11:1-4. As we said earlier, mankind knew that they were created in the image of God and they also knew the principle of coming to God His way. In the process of time, man began to do their own thing and no longer came to God His way in order to maintain their relationship with Him as Romans 10:3 states, *"For they being ignorant of God's righteousness, and **going about to establish their own righteousness**, have not submitted themselves unto the righteousness of God"* (emphasis mine). The New Life Version states this verse in this manner, *"They have not known how God makes men right with Himself. Instead, they have tried to make their own way. They have not done what God said to do"*. Again, they began to do things their own way and make up their own values, morals and standards of living. They discontinued their relationship with God.

Mankind had set out to establish their own way of being right. The account in Genesis 11 is more than a Sunday school story: it is an event that records a key turning point in mankind's history in matters of rebellion against God Himself by man's own devices. This foolishness had settled in the heart of man to the extent that man would begin to do things their way and it continues to this day. Mankind had revolted. Obviously, once again, by this point in man's history, relationship with God was discontinued as man refused to come to God His way.

THREE DYNAMICS TOOK PLACE AT THE TOWER OF BABEL:

1st, we see the attempt of an organized religion (the religion of man) "*let us build a tower to heaven*" - the underlying attitude is that which says, "*I will come to God and reach heaven through my way.*" Or that which says, "*I will find my own way.*"

2nd, we see that by saying, "*let us make a name for ourselves*" reveals the underlying attitude that mankind wants his own identity - they no longer want to be identified with God which was inherent in man being made in God's image. Instead, they want to create their own image through making a name for themselves. They seek their own significance and importance. Pride begins to manifest outwardly.

3rd, "*let us build ourselves a city... lest we be scattered abroad over the face of the whole earth.*" We see mankind devising their own plan for world power. They independently chose to stay in one place, which was also in direct disobedience to God's original instructions. The desire to rule and have dominion on the earth was no longer under the influence of God's rule. The original instructions given to man are found in Genesis 1:28 and Genesis 9:1 where man was told to "*be fruitful, multiply and fill the earth*". Mankind did not want to fill the earth, instead they wanted to remain in one place and build a kingdom but not under God's rule.

The underlying attitudes that were set in motion by these dynamics which continue in mankind's history to this very day. However, God's Word never changes. His plan always come to pass. We see in the account of Genesis 11 that man did not want to fill the earth. They wanted to remain in one place. In this part of man's history, they no longer wanted to be identified with God and His Kingdom. They wanted their own kingdom. By revolting, they chose their own plan, their own identity, and their own form of worship. These attitudes that have manifested at the tower of Babel infiltrates various and numerous protocols within the culture of man such as:

morals, values, worldview, traditions, customs and religious beliefs, etc. All these eventually leading mankind away from the truth of the knowledge of God and right standing relationship with God.

Again, as said earlier, that according to man's history in their relationship with God, man no longer wanted to be identified with God, man began do their own thing. We then need to ask the following question: do these influences within the protocol of man's culture give us a proper understanding of God and His standard of holiness and of His Kingdom? The way to answer that question is to reflect on Jesus' words, *"Seek ye first the Kingdom of God and His Righteousness and all these things shall be added unto you"* (Matthew 6:33, KJV). *"...assuredly, I say to you, unless you are converted and become as little children, you will by no means enter the Kingdom of Heaven"* (Matthew 18:3, NKJV). *"...whoever does not receive the Kingdom of God as a little child will by no means enter it"* (Luke 18:17, NKJV).

It is critical that one becomes as a little child. We cannot enter into the Kingdom of God thinking we know it all. *We* need to be taught the true values of the Kingdom of God. *We* need to learn the principles, morals, protocol and way of worship of the Kingdom of God. *We* need to unlearn what we have held as a way of living life that is not taught in God's Word. It is crucial to understand, that before accepting Christ, we lived by our own convictions, morals and traditions of our ancestors. However, when we have come to the place of accepting Christ as our personal Lord and Saviour, we need to understand that it is us who needs to change and learn a new way of living, worship, and faith. This cannot be done without the study of His Word, *"Your Word is a lamp to my feet and a light unto my path... The entrance of Your words gives light; it gives understanding to the simple"* (Psalm 119:105, 130, NKJV).

Let us now look at God's response to mankind at the tower of Babel...

CHAPTER FIVE

God Sees It All

"The Lord came down… ." Genesis 11:5.

It is important to realize that God was not and is not ignorant of the plans of man. As Proverbs 15:3 states, *"the eyes of the Lord are in every place, keeping watch on the evil and the good"*. In the following verses we read the intervention of God - His response to the building of the tower of Babel - we find that He was not impressed:

> *And the Lord said, 'indeed the people are one, and they all have one language, and this is what they begin to do; now nothing that they propose to do will be withheld from them. Come let us go down and there confuse their language, that they may not understand one another's speech.' So the Lord scattered them abroad from there over the face of all the earth, and they ceased building the city. Therefore its name is called Babel, because there the Lord confused the languages of all the earth; and from there the Lord scattered them abroad over the face of all the earth (Genesis 11:5-9, NKJV).*

In His mercy, He confused their language and He also scattered them across the whole earth. He made sure His plan for man to fill the earth came to pass. He dealt with man like a loving father would deal with his disobedient children. He saw that man's foolishness would only lead them further away from Him. He also gave them what they wanted - their own identity - He confused their language. Consequently, these individuals received their own individual language. In doing so, diverse tongues were dispersed among them thereby receiving their own identity.

Although it was His doing in creating so many languages, it was also an act of judgement in order that man would know who was really in charge. Earlier we mentioned Paul's words, *"He created all the people of the world and from one man, Adam, and scattered the nations across the face of the earth. He decided before hand which should rise and fall and when. He determined their boundaries. His purpose in all this is that they should seek after God and perhaps feel their way toward Him and find Him"* (Acts 17:26-27, T.L.B.). God's intent was that man would not only realize that they were to be under His rule and follow His agenda but that man needs to repent and seek the Lord.

Man needs to seek restitution and continue to come to the Lord His way. In scattering them, they could not influence each other to do their own thing but fear God and seek after Him. They were unable to communicate to each other and carry on in their foolish plan. Although they each now received a new language to speak they needed to communicate with God who created their language. It is from these different language groups that various cultures and religions have developed. The questions still remains: *Did they find their own way? Did they find God?*

The remainder of Genesis 11 gives us the rest of the genealogies from Noah's sons and centers in on Shem. Now the story shifts from dealing with man as a whole to one family group, Abram and Sarai the descendants of Shem who were from a place called Haran.

As time progressed, we discover in Genesis that man continued to do his own thing. A case in point would be the account about Sodom and Gomorrah in Genesis 18 where this particular group of people had become so morally corrupt and perverse in their ways. Genesis 18:20-21, God tells Abraham that *"the outcry against them is great and that their sin is very grave"*. God was about to judge these two cities. Abraham intercedes for them and God promises that if He found even ten righteous still living among them, He would not destroy them. But unfortunately, only four were found, Lot and his wife and their two daughters. God always means what He says and He carried out His judgements against both cities (see Genesis 19).

However, lets briefly overview Genesis chapters 12-17. To summarize, we read of how God calls Abram. We learn that Abram and Sarai had no children. They had no one to inherit their possessions or take on the family name. Yet God had called them and chose them. He also promises them numerous children. So numerous that they could not be numbered. God's purpose in mind was to bring forth the promised Deliverer. As we have learned earlier, that man had become corrupt with a sin nature that continually led mankind into rebellion and going their own way. God had an agenda in mind and that was to deal with the root of mankind's problem. He chose Abram's family line to bring forth the promised Deliverer. Abram means *"exalted father"*[7]. Further in his life (see Genesis 17), we find how God had changed Abram's name to *Abraham* meaning *"father of many nations"*[8].

It was God who gave Abraham a new identity. By changing his identity, He also gave him a new purpose and vision for his life. He revealed to Abraham that the promised Deliverer would come through his blood line. Abraham's grandson, Jacob, also received a new identity. In Genesis 32:22-28, we read how his name was changed to Israel after he wrestled with the angel of the Lord. The name of Jacob was like a curse to him and led him to make many mistakes. His name meant, *"supplanter, underminer, heel catcher"*[9], instead, Jacob was given a new name *Israel* meaning *"God prevails."*[10]. It is God who will intervene and cause His purposes to come forth. God promises Israel that the promised Deliverer would come through his family. God wanted a people for Himself, a people that would walk in His ways and His way is the way of holiness.

IT IS IMPORTANT TO UNDERSTAND THAT:
HOLINESS IS THE ESSENTIAL PART OF GOD'S KINGDOM.

God's desire for the people of Israel was that they become an example of coming to God His way. At this point in man's history, man obviously had lost their way as a blind man who could not find his way unless he is guided by a trusted leader. Therefore, God's plan began to come forth and He appointed Israel to be set apart for His purposes in order that the promised Deliverer would come.

Why did God wait so long? I believe it was that man would realize their true spiritual condition and desperation for a true Saviour. They needed to know or realize that they needed to be delivered from sin and to become desperate to be made right with God.

Isaiah 9:6 foretells of this coming Saviour and reminds Israel that promised Deliverer who is coming will deliver all of mankind from sin and that this promised Deliverer is coming through their people. By revelation, Isaiah indicates the kingly attributes of this promised Deliverer, *"the government shall be upon His shoulders"*. Daniel 2:44 also speaks of His Kingdom which shall have no end. This is speaking of a spiritual kingdom, the realm of God that will invade man's kingdom and break the powers of darkness which influences man's kingdom. As prophesied by Isaiah over 800 years before it happened, Jesus came, born of a virgin (see Isaiah 7:14).

It came to pass! We read the account of this promised Deliverer's natural birth in Matthew 1 and Luke 2.

As we read through the Gospels of Matthew, Mark, Luke and John of Jesus' life and ministry; we find how often He spoke of the Kingdom of Heaven/God. In His night time conversation with Nicodemus, Jesus told him the secret to entrance into the Kingdom of God, *"except a man be born again, he cannot see the Kingdom of God"* (John 3:3, KJV). The key to becoming born again is to believe on Him as He explains in John 3:16-18.

Nicodemus was a teacher of the law, yet he was blinded to the reality of his spiritual condition. He did not understand that the Kingdom of God is a spiritual kingdom and that it was his spiritual condition that prevented him from entering God's Kingdom. Jesus was teaching Nicodemus the point that he was missing. Even though he followed the law of God, as given through Moses, it was not enough. Rather, it was in being born again as he received God's only Son. No amount of good works were able to make him acceptable to God because as Romans 3:23 tells us that all have sinned and fallen short of the glory of God. The concern of God is that we must believe in His Son in order to be saved from spiritual death, the very consequence of sin.

After Jesus suffered and died in our place, as was foretold by the prophets including Isaiah (see Isaiah 53), He arose and conquered death (see Isaiah 25:7, 8 and Hosea 13:14, Psalm 16:10, Luke 24:1-8, 36-43 and John 20). He came to redeem and restore mankind to its original state and make them citizens of Heaven - His Kingdom. This was on the condition that each one simply repent of their sin, believes on His Name and trusts Him for salvation and deliverance from sin. When we believe and accept Jesus as our only Saviour, there is a spiritual dynamic that takes place. Colossians 1:13-14 states that God has, *"...delivered us from the power of darkness and hath translated us into the Kingdom of His dear Son in whom we have redemption through His blood, even the forgiveness of sin"* (KJV). We have become a part of His Kingdom! Not just after we physically die but NOW! Now, while we still have breath, as we live on this earth, we learn to live according to ways of His Kingdom. We begin to learn what it is to be identified with His Kingdom.

Jesus told His followers, including His followers today, that being a part of His Kingdom includes kingdom labour while we are on this earth. We are told, *"go ye into all the world and preach the Gospel to every creature"* (Mark 16:15, KJV). He also goes on to say, *"He that believes and is baptized shall be saved; but he that believes not shall be damned"* (Mark 16:16, KJV). It is our responsibility to share the message of the Gospel. It is not our responsibility if those we speak to choose not to believe, however, for those who do believe, we can rejoice that they too have become a new citizen of Heaven.

Before Jesus ascended into Heaven, He commanded His disciples, *"tarry ye in Jerusalem, until ye be endued with power from on high"* (Luke 24:49, KJV). Acts 1:4, 5 continues the story as He commanded them to, *"wait for the promise of the Father... for John truly baptized with water; but ye shall be baptized with the Holy Ghost not many days hence".*

The disciples ask the question, *"wilt thou at this time restore again the kingdom to Israel?"* (Acts 1:6, KJV). We see in their asking, that they also missed the whole point of why Jesus came. They knew that Jesus was the promised Deliverer and that He is also the King of His Kingdom which He so often taught about. As King, He came to deliver mankind from sin. But they did not yet perceive the reality of the spiritual aspect of His Kingdom, therefore, He commanded them to wait for the promise of the Father.

His Kingdom is a kingdom of His presence - His Holy Spirit, which was how it was in the beginning.

This gives us insight as to why He taught us to pray *"Thy Kingdom come, thy will be done on earth as it is in heaven..."* (Matthew 6:10, KJV). This part of the Lord's prayer ought to clue us in to the fact that life is no longer about our ways, our culture, traditions or religions. Life is no longer about us. It is about Him. *Our significance and identity becomes centered in Christ and His Kingdom.*

CHAPTER SIX

Life Is Not About Us

We read in Acts 1:8, how Jesus tells His disciples that they will receive power after that the Holy Ghost had come upon them and that they would be witnesses unto Him throughout the whole world. The Holy Spirit would be the One who would teach them and redefine who they were and give them a renewed vision and purpose for their lives. He would also give them the power to be witnesses unto Him. The word *witness* in this scripture is to be a *martyr*; where our life is no longer about us but instead it is about Him. Whether we live as dead to the self-life or literally lay down our lives physically, we live unto the purposes of God, *"and He died for all, that those who live should live no longer for themselves, but for Him who died for them and rose again"* (2 Corinthians 5:15, NKJV).

Jesus, in effect, was telling His disciples that they too would lay down their lives; that their lives would become more and more about His Kingdom. By becoming His followers, they now take on a new identity - a Christ-like one; a Christian. *"Therefore, if any man be in Christ, he is a new creature: old things are passed away; behold, all things are become new"* (2 Corinthians 5:17, KJV). ALL THINGS become new!

Acts 2:1-4 gives the account of the fulfillment of this when the Holy Spirit was poured out as also prophesied by Joel (see Joel 2:28-32). It is recorded that the believers who obeyed Jesus' instruction to tarry in Jerusalem and wait for the promise of the Father spoke in other tongues as the Holy Spirit was poured out. They received the gift of speaking in tongues (heavenly and earthly tongues unknown to the speaker). Praying in the spirit is another term used for praying in tongues according to Romans 8:26-27 which enables us to talk to God in prayer when we do not know how to pray. By receiving the gift of the Holy Spirit, believers are empowered to be witnesses unto Him and to do mighty works in His Name.

Paul related that his identity was based on who he was - a servant of Christ. Before his conversion, his name was Saul (See Acts 13:9), which means *"desired"*[11] and his new name was changed to Paul, meaning *"small"*[12]. It was no longer about him, but about Jesus. He also related that he was called to be an apostle; and that the purpose of his calling was to be separated unto the Gospel of God (see Romans 1:1). Paul was not ashamed to proclaim this Gospel because he recognized that the message of the Kingdom of God was (and still is) the power of God unto salvation to all who would believe (see Romans 1:16). He also says, *"The life that I now live, I live by the faith of the Son of God..."* (Galatians 2:20, KJV). In other words, what he is saying is, "My life is no longer about me; it is not about trying to find my life - who I am, and what I'd like to do." Paul understood that as a follower of Jesus, life is about Jesus and His Kingdom. This same mindset must become the mindset of all of the followers of Jesus today, as we grow into the understanding that life is not about ourselves. Jesus said, *"...whoever will lose his life for my sake shall find it..."* (Matthew 16:25, KJV). In Mark He says more, *"...for my sake and the gospel's..."* (Mark 8:35b, KJV). His Kingdom becomes our identity as we believe in Him, seek first His Kingdom and forsake the pursuits of this world and follow Him.

We need to understand, that in spite of this ongoing saga of man attempting to find his own identity, significance, purpose, and meaning in life, God had already established a way for man to regain his original identity, purpose, and meaning in life. It is through the revelation of Jesus that we are no longer lost and searching for significance in this world and no longer without God's presence. Throughout millenniums of time, God has been seeking relationship with man, bringing man into right relationship with Him, and showing man how to approach God His way. He has spoken through His prophets and His people and has given His law (His standards of righteousness). He has given us His Son and the scriptures to teach us His way. Jesus said, *"I am the way, the truth, and the life; no man cometh to the Father except by me"* (John 14:6, KJV). Earlier we started out with Hebrews 1:1-2b, *"Long ago God spoke in many different ways to our fathers through the prophets (in visions, dreams and even face to face), telling them little by little about His plans. But now in these days He has spoken to us through His Son..."* (T.L.B.).

Time and time again throughout history, mankind has gone its own way, wanting to do its own thing. Because of this many have truly lost their way. This brings us back to what Paul said, *"...the living God, who made the heaven, the earth, and the sea, and all things that are in them, who in bygone generations allowed all nations to walk in their own ways. Nevertheless He did not leave them without a witness..."* (Acts 14:15b-17a, NKJV). First of all, this verse read that in bygone generations God allowed all nations to walk in their own way, yet He did not leave them without a witness. In other words, He left witnesses - ones who would show the way to those who would choose to obey God's way. However, if there were those who chose not to believe and continue to do their own thing, they were allowed freedom of choice although not choosing God's way put them in a place of not being accepted into His Kingdom on earth and also in heaven. Both choices had eternal consequences. God did not force them to follow His way, yet, He would not leave man an excuse to say they did not know.

Earlier I mentioned three common denominators, let us now look at another one of those common denominators - the subject of religion. In short, religion is another way that mankind identifies himself which often has much to do with what culture-language speaking group one is from. Therefore religion has been linked to man's identity...

CHAPTER SEVEN

Christianity And Religion

It was on a certain weekend where a group of us gathered at breakfast to have a time of sharing. Three main issues for a couple of ladies who were among us that were new to the faith, were discussed: The ritual of the rosary, the traditional Native way of praying and the residential school experience. The ritual of the rosary was taught to them at school and the traditional native way of praying was taught to them at home by the elders. Both ladies could acknowledge the difference their new found faith in Jesus had made for them. They expressed how they now had a peace and a hope that nothing else could offer.

One of the ladies began to share why she used to hate her name. It was given to her by the Priest in the community she grew up in. She related that she no longer hated her name because she realized that God chose her name not the Priest. The very fact that her name was unique in itself made her realize how special her name way. As she began to share about the pain she still felt from the abuse she experienced at the residential school, it was almost as if she got lost in the memories of her past at the kitchen table. Silence fell among everybody as she attempted to pull herself together all the while trying not to break down with tears of sorrow. Silence. One lady gave a scripture out of Isaiah 53 to point to Jesus as the answer for not only understanding our pain as human beings, but that He also bore our grief's and our sorrows. Another also responded to her. It seemed that no matter what people said to try to comfort her, it was to no avail.

As I sat there with them at the kitchen table, it seemed as I listened to these ladies share their struggle between their new found faith in Christ and what they had known all their lives, that somehow answers became clear to me. I had been asking the Lord to show me why we as human beings crave religious prayers and the ritualistic traditions of our culture in light of religion. Now it all made sense - whether it was native religion or another, all fall under one category called *religion*. That's it!

What is the very attempt of religion? To make one's self right with God to correct an inward problem; to make what is wrong right. What is wrong? When I mean wrong, I am indicating that we have been wronged and we have caused wrong.

The religion of man is synonymous with the actions of Adam and Eve where they made coverings of fig leaves for themselves to cover their nakedness. Both Adam and Eve knew that something went wrong after they had disobeyed God's instruction to not eat of the fruit from the tree of knowledge of good and evil. Religion therefore attempts to correct that which is wrong. For instance, a religious/traditional prayer done repetitively cannot take away the pain and anguish of being wronged. Yet, we as human beings feel that *we* must do something to make it right. We feel like we need to *do* something to make healing happen. If our efforts do not satisfy then we look for something else to do it for us - perhaps there is some other ritual we could seek to perform in order to ensure this deeply needed peace and assurance we desire.

In reality, healing and cleansing are what we seek. If healing is not found in order to take away the pain we carry, we seek another solution to provide release. Unfortunately, some have been lost to alcoholism, drug addiction, gambling, addiction to work, sleeping, etc. We do this until the day comes, when the Light of Life - Jesus Christ comes into our life and then things become progressively clearer. We find what we have been looking for, the answer has come! This is the difference between Christianity and Religion.

Religion is about people always seeking to make something right. In Christianity, Jesus paid the price to make it right for those who will receive it. Christ has done what religion cannot do for us and that is to set things right, and we as believers in Christ endeavor to walk out in our daily lives that which we have attained in Christ. According to the Word of God, Jesus paid it all. Jesus made the way for us. Jesus bore our pain, our sorrow, our grief, our sickness, our infirmities, and our shame as well as our sin.

In light of Christianity, it was already done for us; therefore there is nothing more for us to *do* other than to receive God's love, forgiveness, mercy and healing. We begin to walk with Him who loves us and to seek first His Kingdom and His righteousness (see Matthew 6:33). It is through this that we begin to find our healing and our true identity.

Religion teaches that you have to *do* something in order to have Godly peace and contentment. Christianity teaches, according to the Word of God, that Christ did it for us and only what He has done satisfies both the heart of God and man - that is if man will accept His way. Religion is based on *what we* perceive *we know* and *what we do*, whereas Christianity is based on *who* we know - Jesus and what *He done for us and will do through us.*

Healing is found in the finished work of the cross. Peace is found in the finished work of the cross. Mercy is found in the finished work of the cross. Forgiveness is found in the finished work of the cross. Since this is so, would it also be true that our identity as believers' is found in the finished work of the cross? That is why Jesus clearly states, *"I am the way, the truth and the life, no man cometh to the Father except by me"* (John 14:6, KJV). Jesus also states, *"If ye continue in my word, then are ye my disciples indeed; and ye shall know the truth, and the truth shall make you free"* (John 8:31b-32, KJV).

On the weekend spoken of earlier, the first person who responded to the lady sharing the grief of her abuse, referred to Isaiah 53. If we truly read through that passage of scripture we would see how powerful it is. It is a prophecy which foretold of Jesus, clarifying the very purpose of why He had come to this lost and dying world. The purpose Jesus came was to pay the price of sin; sin that we have committed and sin that others have committed against us. Jesus came to make it right. He came to give us life, an abundant life - eternal life. He came to give us healing both spiritually, emotionally and physically. We only need to receive and rest in what He has done for us and appropriate it by thanking Him for what He has done.

Why does mankind struggle with the message of the cross? Because of the fact that one has to simply accept what Jesus did for us; no "if's", "ands", or "buts". It is not what we can do to make ourselves good enough or what we can do to heal ourselves. It all rests on what Jesus, through His great love, has already done for us. We need to only believe and receive it by faith. As humans, we find it hard to believe that Jesus paid it all, yet when we make the choice to believe it is so, we come to the first step of our healing process through the finished work of the cross. Jesus also completes the healing process within us, as long as continue to trust in Him and the work that He has done; we must receive it and then we walk in it.

As believers in Christ, we now identify ourselves with Christ who was crucified, buried and rose from the dead. *"We are new creations indeed"* (2 Corinthians 5:17, Amp)

CHAPTER EIGHT

There Is A "Cult" In Culture

Jesus knew that as His followers we would face rejection, persecution, scorning and reviling as a result of following Him. He tells us how to handle it:

> *You are blessed when people hate you, when they exclude you, insult you, and slander your name as evil because of the Son of Man. "Rejoice in that day and leap for joy! Take note – your reward is great in heaven, for this is the way their ancestors used to treat the prophets. ... "But I say to you who listen: Love your enemies, do what is good to those who hate you, bless those who curse you, pray for those who mistreat you. If anyone hits you on the cheek, offer the other also. And if anyone takes away your coat, don't hold back your shirt either. Give to everyone who asks you, and from one who takes your things, don't ask for them back. Just as you want others to do for you, do the same for them. If you love those who love you, what credit is that to you? Even sinners love those who love them. If you do what is good to those who are good to you, what credit is that to you? Even*

sinners do that. And if you lend to those from whom you expect to receive, what credit is that to you? Even sinners lend to sinners to be repaid in full. But love your enemies, do what is good, and lend, expecting nothing in return. Then your reward will be great, and you will be sons of the Most High. For He is gracious to the ungrateful and evil. Be merciful, just as your Father also is merciful. (Luke 6:22-23; 27-36, HCSB).

Now therefore, as new creatures of the Kingdom of God we are confronted with the pressures of this world to conform to the cultures of this world which we are surrounded by. We come to find that the protocol - morals, values and beliefs of the Kingdom of God are different from those of the world we live in. When relating with others who are not of the same faith to that of Jesus Christ, we are confronted with a choice to either please the other or choose to please God. We start to realize that their values, convictions, view points, and even customs of the world are not so agreeable with the Word of God. We realize that God's Word has revealed that they cannot be blended with one another (see Deuteronomy 18:9, Ezekiel 44:23, Malachi 3:18).

When one comes into a culture different from their own they experience what is termed "culture shock". Even so within their own culture, with which they grew up with (apart from the influence of the Kingdom of God), there is a risk of offending our own when we don't meet those cultural expectations. One example might be not going home for Christmas to be with your family, when God has you called to be in another place during that time. The value of being about your Heavenly Father's business takes priority over the value of being with your family. The family will either respect how God has called you or they will pressure you to go against what you know of how God has led you. That pressure is what I mean when I say "there is a cult in culture".

A more specific example in light of protocol: I was asked to help with music and singing at a certain place of worship for a funeral service. After having not been in this kind of place in many years, I forgot what the protocol was as you enter this building before you sit down. I went straight to the spot where I was to be seated with my guitar and music sheets and started immediately setting up so that I would not delay any time when I was called upon to sing at the moment's notice.

One of the people sitting in the crowd glared at me with a frown. I didn't know what for. I then saw that every person before they went to take their seat would give a sign and then bow to a certain image that was at the front of the building before they sat down first. I recalled at that moment, this is what I used to do as a little girl when we would go to this place of worship and attended funerals in the same building. I then realized why I was being frowned at. However, the Word of God reveals that we are not to bow down to any image (see Exodus 20:4-5). Because I know what the Word of God says, then it is during this time that I choose to follow God's Word and not the protocol of culture and/or religious tradition.

A year later, I was asked to come again to that same place to help with music and singing for another funeral. As I walked into the building with my guitar and song book, I remembered the protocol before you sit down and proceed any further. I walked over to the left side where I was not in front of that image and continued to make my way over to my delegated spot. This way, I believe, that I was not being offensive, yet I did not compromise the Word of God.

How do we find our way and why do we believe what we believe in this world we call earth that at this point in mankind's history has seemed to be so disoriented, dysfunctional and unsatisfying? We the find the answer in Matthew 6:33 which tells us to *"seek first the Kingdom of God and His righteousness"*.

The truth of the matter is, *we* cannot find our way. We - mankind have tried to find our own way. We tried to do it without God. In fact, man's journey, apart from God, has gone into such a downward spiral to the point that some believe that the One Who created them does not exist and have set themselves on a course to prove it. Romans 1:18-32 gives us very clear picture of this. Let's look at what it says:

> *God's anger is revealed from heaven against every ungodly and immoral thing people do as they try to suppress the truth by their immoral living. What can be known about God is clear to them because*

he has made it clear to them. From the creation of the world, God's invisible qualities, his eternal power and divine nature, have been clearly observed in what he made. As a result, people have no excuse. They knew God but did not praise and thank him for being God. Instead, their thoughts were pointless, and their misguided minds were plunged into darkness. While claiming to be wise, they became fools. They exchanged the glory of the immortal God for statues that looked like mortal humans, birds, animals, and snakes.
(Romans 1:18-23, GW).

The heart of the matter among those who claim there is no existence of God, is that they are in effect saying to themselves *"If I can prove that God does not exist then I can live conscious free and live how I please."* Others have simply kept themselves distant from any type of religion that man has created in order to stay conscious free and yet others still choose to believe that there is a God. However, there are whole societies given to the conviction that disorder breeds disruption and chaos; and therefore the necessity of holding a society to a certain set of values, rules and traditions and religious rites will help to maintain the balance of life given to us by the Creator. There is nothing wrong with the concept of this, but the question remains: *What gives them the guiding principles to govern by? Is it from the Word of God?*

When Jesus was on this earth, representing God to mankind, He made an impacting statement that caused so much upset among a society filled with numerous ethnic groups and in particular, His own people - the Jews. What was his statement? He said, *"I am the way, the truth and the life"* (John 14:6). How could this be possible? That one could claim to be something so absolute and divine is outlandish. After all, hadn't we found our way? For the Jews it was, didn't *we* have the way?

Jesus *is* the way. What an interesting statement to say that He is the way and then to proceed with the thought that He is also the truth and the life. Yet why, when He made this clear statement did it cause such angry reactions to those who felt they knew the way? How about today? The reason is because the statement Jesus made indicated that He was God. He could make that statement because it was the truth - He was and is God. Only God could claim to be THE way, THE truth and THE life - the very three aspects that mankind set out to find and claim for themselves.

For others, upon hearing Jesus' words, something must have come clear to those who were sincerely searching, *"Yes, I have been searching all this time and He is the One who found me and showed me the way."* The search is over and now all that has to be done is to believe, accept and trust in Jesus as the only way, truth and life. How wonderful it is to discover that the very One Who created us came to rescue us - mankind - even after we deliberately turned against Him to do our own thing. He came to show us the way.

God in His mercy, saw that mankind was only going further and further away from the truth and further and further away from Him. It was He who intervened and sent Jesus to not only reveal the Father to us, but to also deliver and rescue us from our own path of destruction. Jesus came to re-establish the Kingdom of God *in the hearts of mankind* which could never be destroyed or corrupted. His Kingdom is a kingdom of truth and righteousness.

LONG AGO GOD SPOKE...

Long ago God spoke in many different ways to our fathers through the prophets (in visions, dreams and even face to face), telling them little by little about His plans. But now in these days He has spoken to us through His Son to whom He has given everything and through whom He made the world and everything there is. God's Son shines out with God's glory and all that God's Son is and does marks Him as God. He regulates the universe by the mighty power of His command. He is the One who died to cleanse us and clear our record of all sin, and then sat down in the highest honour beside the great God of heaven (Hebrews 11:1-3, T.L.B).

Long ago God spoke...
- in many different ways
- To our fathers

- Through His prophets, in visions, dreams and even face to face.

But now in these days He has spoken to us through His Son...
- Jesus is as God is.
- He is the very express image of God
- God speaks to us of Who He is and who we are through His Son

The only way to fully embrace the values of His Kingdom is that we must leave our own "world" of ideas, lifestyle and convictions. When this begins to happen, the cult in the culture of this world will no longer be able to successfully pressure or manipulate believers to re-conform to the old way. We must accept the fact that as believers and followers of Christ, we will face persecution. Persecution comes in some form or another. Jesus warned his followers about it (see John 15:20). Instead of going into a pity party over being persecuted, we can bless and pray for those who are doing the persecuting (see Matthew 5:11; 5:44, Romans 12:14). It is during this pressure that we make our choice to still keep following Christ, seek to please Him and all that He stands for.

If we compromise in order to make other's "happy" with us for fear of what "they" will think of us or do to us, is when we realize we have not fully taken up our cross to follow Jesus. People who are doing the persecuting are not our enemies. We must realize that they do not know Jesus. They are under the influence of this world and not the Kingdom of God. It is more important to be concerned about pleasing God no matter what consequences this world will put us through. God see's it all and we will answer to Him; so will they.

Earlier we mentioned Abraham, who God called out of his kindred, his father's house and country (see Genesis 12:1). The word *kindred* from the Hebrew word means "*nationality, lineage, native country, also offspring, family*"[13]. We see that God called him out from the place he had grown up, what he had always known. He was called out of his comfort zone. At that point in his life, his original name was Abram.

I've often wondered, did Abram think he was to seek another religion, or another culture? Hebrews 11:8 confirms that *"he went out not knowing where he was going"*. He simply heard God calling him and he followed God, yet where was this God whom he had not yet known taking him to? After all, he came from a culture filled with idolatry and its own protocol - philosophy of life, world-view and religious beliefs. Genesis 12:1 speaks of a land that God would show him. The word *land* speaks of "a country or state"[14]. Hebrews 11:10 confirms that, *"he waited for the city which has foundations, whose builder and maker is God"* (NKJV).

Yet, God called him out of all that he was familiar with to know Him. God did not call Abram to another religion. He called him out to know Him. God did not call Abram out to *form* another religion or another culture either. He called him out to Know Him. Perhaps Abram, living within a land filled with paganism, yearned for something more than what he was surrounded with. Perhaps he came from a well-to-do- upbringing and his own inherited religion just could not meet the void he felt inside. Perhaps he searched and tried to be as righteous as he could as a man of integrity yet still something was missing. Whatever the case for Abram, God called him out and he simply responded to His bidding. God wanted Abram to know Him and His plan was that through Abram's life He would be known.

Often it is our own cultural upbringing that causes us to misrepresent the Kingdom of God because we venture out with the values of the culture of which we are familiar with and not that of the Kingdom of God. We have not understood the values the Kingdom of God. It is rather unfortunate that many of those who have followed Christ, who set out to represent him in hopes of bringing others into His Kingdom have ended up misrepresenting Him. Perhaps the influence of their culture which they have come from has been the superior rule in their lives rather than that of the values of Christ's Kingdom.

For example: a secular humanistic view manifested through a "me and my needs first" mentality rather than laying down our lives for Him. This influence had hindered them stepping across cultural barriers in order to make Christ truly known to the people that surround them. The values of their culture have different priorities from the values of God's Kingdom and therefore they cannot see past their own culture. This causes them to become ineffective in their station as Christ's representatives.

On the other hand, for others who intend to represent Christ, perhaps the sin that has tainted their character and behaviour prior to entering His Kingdom has not been truly dealt with and they set out to represent Christ and Kingdom before God's time. Perhaps in their immaturity and haste they end up doing the unthinkable; failing miserably and as a result devastating others' faith in Christ. Why is this so?

I believe it is because 1 Peter 3:15 tells us to sanctify the Lord God in your heart. They were more concerned about themselves rather than value the essential part of the Kingdom which is holiness in every aspect of our lives. Paul instructs Timothy not to put a novice in the office or a position of authority lest through pride they fall (see 1 Timothy 3:6). The word *novice* originally meant *"newly planted"*, that is, (figuratively) a *young convert* ("neophyte")[15]: In other words, a novice is simply anyone who is a new believer. It has nothing to do with age but with the spiritual growth and character development of a Christian believer and their ability for teaching doctrine as well as the responsibilities in the ministry and the life of the church. Paul's concern that to put a new believer in the place of leadership in a church too soon is not wise because of the potential for pride causing one's downfall.

Is this why the writer to the Hebrew Christians clearly admonished, *"Looking unto Jesus the author and finisher of our faith"* (Hebrews 12:2, KJV). It takes time for mankind to get it. *Jesus* will not fail us or damage our trust in Him. When we are disappointed we must not forget that although we as people fail, Jesus never will. Each of us must learn to keep pursuing Christ and His way if we want to have life.

Learning His way means following Him and leaving the old ways behind in order to really become a part of His Kingdom and to represent His Kingdom. Our old way of doing things and living and thinking must change to His standard of truth and we must hold to Him, we must hold to the values of His Kingdom and not the values, opinions and/or priorities of our own culture.

This is an amazing process and it is called the transformation of the heart. Paul challenged the Roman Christians to be transformed by the renewing of their minds and be not conformed to the pattern of this world so that they would know what is that good and acceptable will of God (see Romans 12:1). We cannot know the way, the truth and the life that is in Christ through the screen of our own cultures for they are of the world. Did Jesus not say to Pilate, *"My Kingdom is not of this world..."* (John 18:36, KJV)? If we really want to know the ways of Christ, then it is wise to seek Him and His Kingdom. We cannot determine Christian values within the context of our cultures. Christian values are determined in the written Word of God.

CHRISTIANITY IS A KINGDOM OF THE HEART WHERE CHRIST MUST FIRST REIGN.

Often it is our own culture that keeps us from seeing the bigger picture. There was a group of Pharisees that questioned Jesus in matters of tradition, *"Then the Pharisees and scribes asked Him 'Why do your disciples not walk according to the tradition of the elders... ."* (Mark, 7:5, NKJV). Jesus had a wise response to the heart of the matter regarding their traditions, *"...Well, did Isaiah prophesy of you hypocrites, as it is written, 'This people honors Me with their lips, But their heart is far from Me. And in vain they worship Me, teaching as the doctrines the commandments of men.' For laying aside the commandment of God, you hold the tradition of men... All too well you reject the command of God, that you may keep your tradition... making the word of God of no effect through your tradition which you have handed down. And many such things you do"* (Mark 7:6-8a, 9b, 13, NKJV).

Like the Pharisees, mankind loves the practice of tradition, be it cultural or religious. This is considered a work of the flesh where we feel that our efforts give us a sense of being righteous - righteous in accordance with man's tradition that is, but not the righteousness of God. Jesus wanted the Pharisees including those listening (as well as you and I today), to realize that often our own traditions get in the way of our following the ways of the Lord. They blind us from understanding His heart and being all that God wants us to be.

Outside of Christ, Christianity is often viewed as another religion. What mankind doesn't understand is that Christianity was never meant to be another religion, but rather, a way of life which stems from knowing Jesus and living His reality in our lives. The Kingdom of God shows us the way to be free from corruption and healed of our diseases and emotional wounds. It shows us the way of forgiveness and humility. It shows us the standards of purity and integrity. It teaches us to love the unlovely, to touch the untouchable, to pray for those who persecute you, and to bless those who curse you.

Yet most of all, Christianity *enables you to know God*. Therefore if you want to know God, then you must follow Christ because surely He is the way, the truth and the life. It is a matter of believing from your heart and accepting His forgiveness and walking out His grace. It takes time. But don't take too long. Do it before it is too late. Don't allow the pressures of your culture to influence your decision away from Him.

Culture stems from our relationship with people among whom we are brought up with or have come to be a part of. Whereas *Christianity stems from a relationship with Jesus* and this relationship influences how we relate with others as we seek first His Kingdom and His righteousness. Be free in who God made you to be and that is, to know Him, to choose to obey Him and to love Him.

In forming that relationship with Him, we do so on His terms and trust that He will lead us into all truth (see John16:23). This develops into finding our true identity as a child of God as citizens of His Kingdom whom He created in His image. We discover that we are called to be separated unto Him and through him we walk in healing, wholeness and in the power and presence of God to fulfill His plan and call upon our lives.

Upon accepting Christ, our whole sense of value and worth changed at the moment we become born again. Having a born-again experience as we accept Jesus and what He has done on the cross for us is a supernatural encounter that none can explain, yet it is very critical in finding who we really are and Who God originally created us to be (see 2 Corinthians 4:1-7).

But we all, with unveiled face, beholding as in a mirror the glory of the Lord are being transformed into the same image from glory to glory, just as by the Spirit of the Lord (2 Corinthians 3:18, NKJV).

CHAPTER NINE

Spiritual Authority Is Two-Fold

PART ONE

*Therefore if any man be in Christ, he **is a new creature:** old things are passed away; behold**, all things are become new.** And all things are of God, who hath reconciled us to himself by Jesus Christ, and hath given to us the ministry of reconciliation; To wit, that God was in Christ, reconciling the world unto himself, not imputing their trespasses unto them; and **hath committed unto us the word of reconciliation.** Now then **we are ambassadors for Christ**, as though God did beseech you by us: we pray you in Christ's stead, be ye reconciled to God. For he hath made him to be sin for us, who knew no sin; **that we might be made the righteousness of God in him***
(2 Corinthians 5:17-21, KJV, emphasis mine).

AMBASSADORS FOR CHRIST

As new creations in Christ, God has also given us a new purpose, a mandate to fulfill and renewed vision for our lives. His Word tells us that we are *ambassadors for Christ*. What has been committed to our trust is the *word of reconciliation* – a calling of the world to make it right with God through the acceptance His Son. A person functioning in the role of an ambassador only speaks the mind of his ruling leader whom he is sent to represent in another country. He speaks on behalf of his leader and speaks only what his leader would speak.

This is an area in ministry where, I believe, many have missed the mark. They go representing Jesus but do not speak *His* Word. Instead, they give a compromised message of the gospel and thereby many are deceived and led astray. An ambassador is never to speak of his own opinion or do of his own interest's whenever he is sent to represent his country and to speak on behalf of his leader. He is required and trusted to only be mindful of the business of his country and speak only what he knows his leader would speak. This takes relationship. How can one know the mind of their leader without being in constant communion and relationship with their leader? One would need to learn their leaders' ways, intentions and goals. If this process has not happened, then they would not be able to represent their country properly or speak the mind of their leader on behalf of them.

Do we realize this principle is the same with the Kingdom of God? We have been committed - trusted with - the Word of reconciliation which is another term for the Gospel of Christ. This is the message we are required to preach – nothing more and nothing less than the pure gospel of Jesus Christ. Where is our sense of conviction and fear of the Lord when it comes to proclaiming His Word? Do we realize how serious an offense we cause Him when we speak our own opinion and not His Word? These words, *word of reconciliation* and *ambassadors for Christ*, were chosen in this set of scriptures not to make us feel important. These words were chosen for us to realize the importance of the task entrusted to us by God. We will answer to God for how we represented Him in this world.

As Christ's ambassadors, we are representing Jesus and His Kingdom; therefore whenever and wherever He sends us, we are also sent with His Divine authority.

OUR POSITION IN CHRIST

If ye then be risen with Christ, seek those things which are above, where Christ sitteth on the right hand of God. Set your affection on things above, not on things on the earth. For ye are dead, and your life is hid with Christ in God. When Christ, who is our life, shall appear, then shall ye also appear with him in glory. Mortify therefore your members which are upon the earth; fornication, uncleanness, inordinate affection, evil concupiscence, and covetousness, which is idolatry: For which things' sake the wrath

of God cometh on the children of disobedience: In the which ye also walked some time, when ye lived in them. But now ye also put off all these; anger, wrath, malice, blasphemy, filthy communication out of your mouth. Lie not one to another, seeing that ye have put off the old man with his deeds; And have put on the new man, which is <u>renewed in knowledge after the image of him that created him</u>: Where there is neither Greek nor Jew, circumcision nor uncircumcision, Barbarian, Scythian, bond nor free: but Christ is all, and in all
(Colossians 3:1-11, KJV, emphasis mine).

When walking in spiritual authority, it is important to understand that our position is in Him, for this is where our confidence rests. Our position of authority is based upon who we are in Christ. Verse 10 states, *"And have put on the new man, which is renewed in the knowledge after the image of Him who created him,"* KJV After the image of who? Jesus! Genesis 1:26-27; 2:7 reveals the beginning of the creation of this image.

And God said, Let us make man in our image, after our likeness: and let them have dominion over the fish of the sea, and over the fowl of the air, and over the cattle, and over all the earth, and over every creeping thing that creepeth upon the earth. So God created man in his own image, in the image of God created he him; male and female created he them..."
"And the LORD God formed man of the dust of the

ground, and breathed into his nostrils the breath of life; and man became a living soul (KJV).

HOW IT WAS IN THE BEGINNING:

At the creation of man, God deposited a likeness of Himself when He breathed into man the breath of life. His breath was the very impartation of His Holy and righteous nature - His *Holy* Spirit. This was that image of which God originally created mankind into. Our bodies are a mere shell - a house with which our spirit and soul live. Our spirit is the very center of who we are, whereas our soul consists of our mind - the place where our thoughts, will, emotions, attitudes and memory functions. It is within our spirit being that God made a deposit of Himself into us. It was a deposit of His holy and righteous nature. This was our original identity - made in the image of God.

At the creation of mankind, Adam and Eve originally walked in God's Divine authority on the earth because they were in subjection to God's authority. He gave man dominion upon the earth (see Genesis 1:26, 28). He gave man the right to name all the animals (see Genesis 2:19-20). Our Creator had given man the right to rule over the earth yet it was to be under His authority. Mankind lived and walked in unity and harmony with God. There was an undivided, respectful and loving relationship between the Creator and His creation. At the beginning of creation, Adam and Eve walked secure in who they were and their God given identity – they were confident knowing that they were made in His image.

What happened to this image of God creation? Or, what happened to our original identity? Genesis 3, tells us of Adam and Eve's act of disobedience. Earlier, we discussed that both Adam and Eve were acting on behalf of the human race. Here is where mankind became separated from God and from His righteous and holy nature of His Holy Spirit. This union between God and man had become breached. It is because of sin that mankind no longer has the likeness of God within them. The spirit of man died because it is sin that brings death. A sin nature took over the inner being of man.

Wherefore, as by one man sin entered into the world, and death by sin; and so death passed upon all men, for that all have sinned (Romans 5: 12, KJV).

The law of nature, as created by God, has always been that each living thing produces after its kind. Apple trees produces apples. Oranges produces oranges. Trees produce trees. Flowers produce flowers. Animals produce animals. Ever since Adam, sinful man produces sinful man. Mankind, now has a sin nature. Mankind also lost the right to have dominion - God's divine authority on the earth. Instead of man having dominion over the earth, man began to worship the things of the earth. They became lost in who they were created to be.

WHAT DID GOD DO TO SOLVE THIS PROBLEM?

> *For God so loved the world, that he gave his only begotten Son, that whosoever believeth in him should not perish, but have everlasting life. For God sent not his Son into the world to condemn the world; but that the world through him might be saved.*
> *(John 3:16, 17, KJV).*

Mankind could do nothing to solve the problem of a sinful nature. No religion or human effort could resolve the issue of sin. It is only because of Jesus and our receiving of Him that we as believers no longer have a sinful nature (see Romans 5:15, 19). John 3:3, Jesus speaks to Nicodemus about being born again. We must become born again in order for us to be restored to our original creation and our original identity as we have been made into His image. This born again experience begins with our first repenting of our sins and accepting Jesus Christ as our only Saviour, Healer and Deliverer.

Colossians 2:13 uses the term, *"quickened together"*; this is another way that Paul used the term born again. At first, because of sin we were dead. *What part of us died?* It was our spirit man. But now, because we have received Christ, we are made alive unto God. We have received a righteous nature in exchange of a sinful nature (see 2 Cor. 5:17). 2 Cor. 5:21 *"For He made Him who knew no sin to be sin for us, that we might become the righteousness of God in Him"*, (NKJV). It's important to understand that through Christ we now have a righteous nature that was imparted to us the moment we became born again.

We do not have two natures in our spirit at work within us. *"When you came to Christ, you were circumcised but not by a physical procedure. Christ performed a spiritual circumcision – the cutting away of your sinful nature... You were dead because of your sins and because your sinful nature was not yet cut away. Then God made you alive with Christ, for He forgave all our sins"* (Colossians 2:11, 13, NLT). God has removed that sin nature from our spirit and He has given us His nature, a new nature and because of this we are born again - made alive unto God. What was lacking (a righteous nature) is now filled. Romans 11:27 *"I will take away their sin"* - the sin problem is resolved at the Cross of Calvary. We are not just forgiven, but now we are made into a new creation.

WHAT IS OUR PART?

We must renew our mind - our soul part needs to learn a new way of living, thinking, believing, behaving and attitude. Our soul needs to learn to agree with the new creation as revealed in the Word of God. Romans 6: 13 speaks of yielding our members as instruments of righteousness. Romans 12:2 speaks of being transformed by the renewing of our mind. Ephesians 4:23 tells us to be renewed in the spirit of our mind.

And have clothed yourselves with the new (spiritual self), which is (ever in the process of being) renewed

> *and remolded into (fuller and more perfect knowledge upon) knowledge after the image (the likeness) of Him Who created it. (Colossians 3:10, Amp).*

> *But grow in grace, and in the knowledge of our Lord and Saviour Jesus Christ... (2 Peter 3:18, KJV).*

We are expected of God to grow in grace and *in the knowledge of* Christ. No longer do we define ourselves according to our ancestry or our history or our past. It is the cross of Christ that now defines who we are. We are that new creation. This is it! This is our new identity; created in the image of God. 2 Cor. 5:17 tells us that old things are passed away, BEHOLD *all things* have become new. BEHOLD that new creation! Paul reminds us of what our sinful selves used to look like and how it behaved before we received Christ (see Galatians 5:19-21). That sinful old self is passed away. He then gives us insight as to what that new creation looks like and how by God's grace we are growing in this new creation:

> *But the fruit of the Spirit is love, joy, peace, long-suffering, kindness, goodness, faithfulness, gentleness self control... (Galatians 5:22-23a, KJV).*

We are not *trying* to be a new creation, rather we already have *been made* that new creation because we have received Christ. He has made us righteous. However, it is our soul that has catch up with this new reality! Our soul must *unlearn* what it learned from the old self-life including all the old patterns of behaviour, thinking and attitudes. Our soul must come into submission to the new creation in our spirit. These qualities (fruits of the Spirit) must be developed. These qualities are nurtured through the Word of God, prayer and worship – our relationship with Jesus. They are developed by putting to action what we are learning about that righteous nature. *"I have been crucified with Christ; it is no longer I who live, but Christ lives in me; and the life which I now live in the flesh I live by the faith of the Son of God, who loved me and gave Himself for me"* (Galatians 2:20, NKJV). We live as new creations in Christ Jesus!

OUR TRUE POSITION OF SPIRITUAL AUTHORITY

He who sins is of the devil, for the devil has sinned from the beginning. For this purpose was the Son of God manifested, that He might destroy the works of the devil (1 John 3:8, KJV).

Jesus came to destroy the works of the devil. He redeemed the human race with His blood from the powers of Satan and all of hell. Jesus destroyed the works of the devil when He died on the cross, was buried and rose from the dead. He shouted on the cross, *"It is finished!"* (see John 19:20). This shout was a victorious and triumphant shout. What an interesting place that Jesus made that victorious shout from.

And you, being dead in your trespasses and the uncircumcision of your flesh, He has made alive together with Him, having forgiven you all trespasses, having wiped out the handwriting of requirements that was against us, which was contrary to us. And He has taken it out of the way, having nailed it to the cross. Having disarmed principalities and powers, He made a public spectacle of them, triumphing over them in it. (Colossians 2:13-15, NKJV, emphasis mine).

When a triumph is made there is often a great shout indicating the victory that has been won. When Jesus shouted on the cross those victorious words, it wasn't from a tiresome place of *"Whew! Glad it's finally done!"* Nor was it from a barely-making-it through kind of victory.

Have you ever watched a football game where the quarter back takes a clean break on the field with the ball tucked under his arm as he runs so freely while his opponents are far behind him? When he gets to the score line on the field and his run is the final winning score of the game, there is a shout along with a jump and maybe a few somersaults. The winning team raises that player up in the air to celebrate the victory as they shout and holler because they won the game. There is a lot of excitement in the air! This is similar, yet even more grand for Jesus when He was on the cross shouting, *"It is finished!"* He was full of zeal and compassion that the devil's works had been destroyed. Therefore you and I who receive the message of the Good news are delivered from the Satan's hands.

Ephesians 2:4-6, tells us that we are seated in heavenly places in Christ Jesus. Jesus said, *"Behold, I give you authority to trample on serpents and scorpions, and over all the power of the enemy, and nothing shall by any means hurt you. Nevertheless do not rejoice in this, that the spirits are subject to you, but rather rejoice because your names are written in heaven"* (Luke 10:19-20, NKJV). Jesus tells us what we are to rejoice in - *that our names are written in Heaven*. It is from this place that we rejoice and it is from this place that we can walk in victory over sin, and Satan and his works. This is our true position of spiritual authority. It is because of *who* we are *in Christ* that we can walk in true spiritual authority. In Him, we are who we are because of *what Jesus accomplished* on the cross for us; we are forgiven of our sins and set free from the grip of the enemy and that is why we are able to walk in victory.

This now leads us on to the second-fold part of our spiritual authority which we have in Christ, and that is we are His *sent one's...*

CHAPTER TEN

Spiritual Authority Is Two-Fold

PART TWO

WE MUST BE IN SUBMISSION TO CHRIST

To have authority, we must be under authority. The apostle James gives key steps in walking in spiritual authority:

But He gives more grace, therefore He says: God resists the proud, But gives grace to the humble. Therefore submit to God. Resist the devil and he will flee from you. Draw near to God and He will draw near to you. Cleanse your hands, you sinners; and purify your hearts, you double-minded (James 4:6-8, NKJV).

Notice our attention is brought to God's grace. This grace is not just a mere free ticket into heaven. Grace by definition is: *the divine influence upon the heart and its reflection in the life with gratitude.*[16] In others words - grace is God's empowerment. But this grace is conditional to our humility and our submission to God. If we are walking in pride, there is no grace available to us. However, if we are in walking in humility, His grace is given to us. Our key to this empowerment is that in humility we submit to God. This speaks of a daily submission of our self-life to God and then we have the power to resist the devil and watch him flee.

The word *submit* comes from the Greek word *hupotassō* (Strong's #5293): to *subordinate*; reflexively to *obey*: - be under obedience (obedient), put under, subdue unto, (be, make) subject (to, unto), be (put) in subjection (to, under), submit self unto[17]

The word *double minded* comes from the Greek word *dipsuchos* (Strong's #1374): *two spirited*, that is, *vacillating* (in opinion or purpose): double minded.[18]

We must come into obedience to God. There cannot be any area of disobedience to God in our lives. That is why we are also exhorted to cleanse our hands and purify our hearts. We cannot be living a double life where we are back and forth in what we believe of God and His Word - living for Jesus or/and then not living for Jesus. Sin, disobedience, and doubt weaken our ability to have power over the devil.

Being able to resist the devil is never without our submission to God first. If we want to walk in victory in our lives we must be in submission to God in every area of our lives. Without submission to God there is no authority over the devil and his works. However, when we are in submission to God and we know who we are in Christ, we can then resist the devil and he will flee. It is then that God's power activates through our lives and destroys the works of darkness.

HE SENDS US, THEREFORE HE BACKS US UP

Now when Jesus had entered Capernaum, a centurion came to Him, pleading with Him, saying, Lord, my servant is lying at home paralyzed, dreadfully tormented. And Jesus said to him, I will come and heal him. The centurion answered and said, Lord, I am not worthy that You should come under my roof. But only speak a word, and my servant will be healed. For I also am a man under authority, having soldiers under me. And I say to this one, 'Go' and he goes; and to another, 'Come' and he comes; and to my servant, 'Do this' and he does it. When Jesus heard it, He marveled, and said to those who followed, assuredly, I say to you, I have not found such great faith, not even in Israel! (Matthew 8:5-10, NKJV).

Often, this passage of scripture is discussed in the matters of having doubtless faith. Jesus was impressed with the faith of this centurion. When you read of the centurion's faith you find that his faith wasn't so much from the perspective of battling unbelief. He makes this key statement that reveals his accurate perception of the release of God's power: Verse 9, "*I am a man under authority...*".

The Centurion understood *how* God's power (His authority) operated *in principle*. In the times of the Roman regime, a centurion was one who was in charge of at least 100 soldiers. A centurion had the Roman government backing him up because He was in submission to the Roman government. He was put in a position of authority under the direction of the Roman government. He understood that the orders he gave to those under his charge was backed up by the Roman government which he represented. The Centurion saw Jesus as one who was under the authority of the Kingdom of Heaven - He saw that Jesus was in submission to God. Because of this, he knew that Heaven would back up the very word Jesus spoke.

This applies to us today. Consider, how Jesus operated in God's power *by the principle of being in submission to God the Father*; we also are to live by that same principle. To have authority we must be under authority. Jesus said, "*I can of mine own self do nothing: as I hear, I judge: and my judgment is just; because* **I seek not mine own will, but the will of the Father which hath sent me**" (John 5:30, KJV, emphasis mine). Again He says, "*... When ye have lifted up the Son of man, then shall ye know that I am he, and* **that I do nothing of myself**; *but as my Father hath taught me, I speak these things*" (John 8:28, KJV, emphasis mine). Also in Matthew, Jesus speaks of only doing the will of the Father: "*Not every one that saith unto me, Lord,*

Lord, shall enter into the kingdom of heaven; but he that doeth the will of my Father which is in heaven" (Matthew 7:21, KJV). And in another place, "*For whosoever shall do the will of my Father which is in heaven, the same is my brother, and sister, and mother*" (Matthew 12:50, KJV). They key is in *doing the will of the Father* not our man-made plans or good intentions.

In fact, if you read through the Gospels, you will find how Jesus not only taught this principle but He lived it all through His life from childhood (see Luke 2:49). It was also seen as He went through the hour of temptation (see Matthew 4:4); in times of emergency (see John 11); when they wanted to make Him a king, He withdrew Himself (see John 6:15). Consider when at the Garden of Gethsamne He chose His Father's will over His own fears (see Matthew 26:29, Luke 22:42, John 18:11); at the cross of Calvary he fulfilled His Father's will (see Luke 23:46, John19:30), and also at His resurrection (see John 20:17).

He then said to His disciples before He ascended into heaven, "*...as the Father has sent Me, I also send you*" (John 20:21, NKJV). Jesus expects nothing less of us. In the same way He was in submission to His Father, He expects us to be in submission to His Father. This is the key to walking in spiritual authority.

CHAPTER ELEVEN
Spiritual Authority Is Progressive

And He went up on the mountain and called to Him those He Himself wanted, and they came to Him. Then He appointed twelve, that they might with be Him and that He might send them out to preach, and to have power to heal sicknesses and to cast out demons (Mark 3:13-15, NKJV).

First of all, they were to be with Him. This speaks of being in relationship with Him. Upon being with Him, He would then send them; because of being with Him they would know where, what, how and who they were being sent to preach. As they were sent to preach, they would have **power** to: heal sicknesses and to cast out devils.

The word *power* in this scripture by definition means to have *delegated influence*. And its synonyms: *authority, privilege, the right, jurisdiction, liberty, right* and *strength*.[19] This spiritual authority (power) was not dependent upon their ancestry, place of birth, ethnic background, education, achievements or anything at all in the flesh or of this world's standards. It was dependent upon their *being with* Jesus and *being sent* by Jesus. If it was important to Jesus that their ancestry or place of birth, etc., was what gave them *jurisdiction*, I believe He would have made it known in scripture. But He gives no such clue, nor the slightest hint that this was of significance or equal value.

Jesus also said, *"...all power is given unto Me in heaven and earth. Go ye therefore and teach all nations, baptizing them in the name of Father, and of the Son, of the Holy Ghost, teaching them to observe all things whatsoever I have commanded you: and lo, I am with you always, even to the end of the world. Amen"* (Matthew 28:18b-20, KJV).

The word *power* by definition means: From the Greek word *exousia* (Strong's # 1832); (in the sense of *ability*); *privilege*, that is, (subjectively) *force, capacity, competency, freedom*, or (objectively) *mastery* (concretely *magistrate, superhuman, potentate, token of control*), delegated *influence: authority, jurisdiction, liberty, power, right, strength*.[20]

The word *nations* by definition means: From the Greek word *ethnos* (Strong's # 1486); a *race* (as of the same *habit*), that is, a tribe; specifically a *foreign* (non-Jewish) one (usually by implication *pagan*): *Gentile, heathen, nation, people*.[21]

Through His delegated influence and authority, Jesus sends His followers to the racial-ethnic groups of which He calls each one to. There is no indication that this authority is conditional on whether or not you were of that same racial background or jurisdiction. The heart of Jesus is to reach souls, no matter the color of one's skin. He died for all and since He did so, He desires that all will hear the Good News. He is looking for those who will *obey* at all costs. He told his disciples before His departure, *"Go into all the world and preach the gospel to every creature. And these signs will follow those who believe: In my Name they will cast out demons; they will speak with new tongues; they will take up serpents; and if they drink anything deadly, it will by no means hurt them; they will lay hands on this sick and they will recover"* (Mark 16:15-18, NKJV).

When He says, "In my Name" He is meaning, in His authority, honor and character. We go representing Him, not ourselves; not our ethnic backgrounds; not our education or status in society. We go representing Him into all the world and we are to proclaim His message to every creature. That means every tribe and tongue will have opportunity to believe and receive the Gospel. This is our mandate. This is where our true spiritual authority rests.

Paul, the apostle, specifically emphasizes the necessity of not having confidence in your lineage of ethnic background, gender or class of society:

> *(In this new creation all distinctions vanish) There is no room for and there can be neither Greek nor Jew, circumcised nor uncircumcised, (nor difference between nations whether alien) barbarians or Scythians (who are most savage of all), nor slave or*

> *free man; but Christ is all and in all (everything and everywhere, to all men, **without distinction of person.**)*
> *(Colossians 3:11, Amp, emphasis mine).*
>
> *... the righteousness of God, through faith in Jesus Christ, to all and on all who believe,. For **there is no difference** (Rom. 3:22, KJV, emphasis mine).*
>
> *There is (now no distinction) neither Jew nor Greek, there is neither slave nor free, there is not male and female; for you are one in Christ Jesus (Galatians 3:28, Amp).*
>
> *Consequently, from now on we estimate and regard no one from a (purely) human point of view (in terms of natural standards of value)... (2 Cor. 5:16, Amp).*
>
> *...and put no confidence or dependence (on what we are) in the flesh and on outward privileges and physical advantages and external appearances. (Philippians 3:3, Amp).*

As far as the Kingdom of Heaven is concerned, there are no status or gender distinctions, nor is there an ethnic emphasis. God views the human race as being in one of two categories: 1) born again or 2) still in a sinful condition. We are either in Christ or not in Christ. We are either a new creation or dead in our sins. Spiritual authority is not dependant on anything we are in our natural status. Therefore our spiritual authority in matters of the Kingdom of Heaven is jointly dependent upon our being born again - made a new creation in Christ and it also is subject to our submission to His Divine authority. It is from that position that He sends us to the places and people He would appoint us to.

BARNABAS AND SAUL

The church at Antioch had several prophets and teachers. They were Barnabas, Simeon, also called Niger, Lucius from Cyrene, Manaen, who was Herod's close friend, and Saul. While they were worshiping the Lord and going without eating, the Holy Spirit told them, "Appoint Barnabas and Saul to do the work for which I have chosen them." Everyone prayed and went without eating for a while longer. Next, they placed their hands on Barnabas and Saul to show that they had been appointed to do this work. Then everyone sent them on their way. After Barnabas and Saul had been sent by the Holy Spirit, they went to Seleucia. From there they sailed to the island of Cyprus. (Acts 13:1-4, CEV).

Notice how Barnabas and Saul were *not self appointed*. They were sent by God as this was confirmed by their spiritual leaders. They were in submission to their leaders under God. They were also sent to a different racial group - ones not of their own kind. In the last few years I have heard much emphasis on how one's ministry needs to wait for a welcoming committee before going into new territory in order to minister the gospel. This kind of thinking is based on a cultural mindset of protocol and traditional custom. It is not based on the authority of God's Word. God's Word is our mandate.

As I was discussing this with a friend of mine, I shared how I could not find this to be a basis of having spiritual authority in the locations of ministry God sends you to. He made this point, *"Jesus had a 'welcoming committee' where they danced Him into Jerusalem, however, the following week that same crowd killed Him"* (see Luke 19:28-40; 23:13-25). As a matter of fact, Jesus spent more emphasis on dealing with being rejected, how that we are to wipe the dust off our feet (see Matthew 10:14, Mark 6:11 and Luke 9:5).

In Acts 13:51, the disciples literally applied his teaching and wiped the dust off their feet. Jesus also taught us how to deal with being mocked, reviled, persecuted and even cursed (see Matthew 5:11-12, 43-48, Luke 6:22-23, 27-36). He warned that we as His followers would also be persecuted as He was (see John 15:20). Jesus knows that this world is under the influence of Satan and because of this, there would be opposition to the work of the Gospel of the Kingdom of Heaven. His emphasis was on how to deal with that opposition when it comes our way. Paul, in Romans 12:14, repeats the same principle, *"Bless them which persecute you; bless, and curse not"* (KJV). Nowhere in the Scriptures does Jesus or any of the apostles give a welcoming protocol for people to adhere to when going to share the gospel.

Barnabas and Saul did not need to wait for a welcoming committee from the people they were sent to before they went. In fact, there were no known believers there to welcome them in first place. Instead, they waited for a Word from the Lord saying, "*Go Ye...*" and in obedience they went. They walked in their God-given (sent authority) and Heaven backed them up. As a result, Paul (formerly known as Saul), raised up numerous churches in these regions that were not of his ancestry. He laboured among a people not of his own race. He used his God-given authority based on his being sent by God and knowing that his mandate came from the command of Jesus saying, "*...Go ye into all the world and preach the Gospel to every creature*" (Mark 16:15, KJV). He did not calculate his spiritual authority as dependent upon his physical lineage or ethnic background, place of birth, etc.

Paul walked in this revelation as he wrote to the believers in Philippi:

Although I once also had confidence in the flesh. If anyone else thinks he has grounds for confidence in the flesh, I have more: circumcised the eighth day; of the nation of Israel, of the tribe of Benjamin, a Hebrew born of Hebrews; regarding the law, a Pharisee; regarding zeal, persecuting the church; regarding the righteousness that is in the law, blameless. But everything that was a gain to me, I have considered to be

a loss because of Christ. More than that, I also consider everything to be a loss in view of the surpassing value of knowing Christ Jesus my Lord. Because of Him I have suffered the loss of all things and consider them filth, so that I may gain Christ and be found in Him, not having a righteousness of my own from the law, but one that is through faith in Christ - the righteousness from God based on faith. My goal is to know Him and the power of His resurrection and the fellowship of His sufferings, being conformed to His death, assuming that I will somehow reach the resurrection from among the dead. Not that I have already reached the goal or am already fully mature, but I make every effort to take hold of it because I also have been taken hold of by Christ Jesus. Brothers, I do not consider myself to have taken hold of it. But one thing I do: Forgetting what is behind and reaching forward to what is ahead, I pursue as my goal the prize promised by God's heavenly call in Christ Jesus. **Therefore, all who are mature should think this way.** *And if you think differently about anything, God will reveal this also to you*
(Philippians 3:4-15, HCSB emphasis mine).

CHAPTER TWELVE
Our Motivation

In many places where I have traveled, I have come to meet numerous people and had become acquainted with various ministries of different nationalities. I have witnessed those who sincerely believe that only they had the right to minister among their own people because they were born of them physically. These same ones have caused great hindrances to the others who were sent by God to minister in their area.

Many have manifested pride, self righteousness and discriminated those not of their skin color, all because of being taught a wrong concept. They believed that those not of their skin color, did not have the right to minister among their people. This is one example of the sour fruit I have seen from these individuals who have accepted this false teaching and it has led them to discriminate others in the body of Christ. It has grieved my heart to witness this kind of behaviour. It has also made me wonder where in scripture do they find the basis of this kind of teaching and the conviction of which they feel is God's Word.

As years have gone by, I have heard several others speak either publicly or to me personally the teaching they heard regarding where our spiritual authority as believers is based. This teaching indicated that our spiritual authority as believers is based on our nationality and place of birth, therefore we are "gate keepers" of the land where we are from. I would hear others share how they firmly believed in this teaching and felt more confident because of it. For some reason this did not sit right in my spirit, yet I would not refute it. I wanted to know *which scripture(s)* was this teaching based on. So I went on a personal search through the Word of God. I have begun to search the scriptures to find some answers, not from the place of trying to prove anyone wrong, but to know for myself: What *does* the Word of God have to say in matters of true spiritual authority?

During my search, I would meet different individuals who used this teaching as a valid reason for their opposition to other ministers of the gospel in their area. This began to be of concern to me, as I began to see the fruit of this teaching was not the fruit of the Spirit as revealed in Galatians 5:22- 23. Jude exhorts believers, "*...to contend earnestly for the faith...*" (Jude 1:3c, NKJV). We are to contend for the faith, not anything else. We are not to contend for our position and place.

The scriptures give us some clear examples regarding our conduct as to how we are to treat other ministries and what our attitude should or should not be like. One example we can look at is Diotrephes. Who was Diotrephes? Sadly, he was noted for his wrong conduct among the brethren. John the apostle reprimanded his behaviour:

> *I wrote to the church, but Diotrephes, who **loves to have the preeminence** among them, does not receive us. Therefore, if I come, I will call to mind his deeds which he does, prating against us **with malicious words**. And not content with that, he himself does not receive the brethren, and forbids those who wish to, putting them out of the church. Beloved do not imitate what is evil, but what is good. But He who does good is of God, but he who does evil has not seen God (3 John 1:9-11, NKJV, emphasis mine).*

The apostle John was grieved by the actions of Diotrephes, revealing the motive as to why He treated fellow workers in the gospel in the way he did. What was his motive? He loved to have the preeminence. That word *preeminence* means *surpassing all others*[22]. In other words, Diotrephes wanted to be more important. Paul tells us of Christ, "*...that in all things He may have the preeminence*" (Colossians 1:18d, NKJV). *Jesus* is the center. He is to have first place. He is the important one! The underlying motive of Diotrephes' behaviour in his malicious words against others appears to be due his envy of them in that he wanted to have first place. Any one who wants to have first place – the pre-eminence – will feel threatened by others who are fellow workers in the Gospel. Often their conduct and attitude toward these fellow workers will be similar to the behaviour of Diotrephes.

This same attitude was a manifestation of Lucifer who was jealous of God and his attempt to overthrow God his Creator. Lucifer manifested an attitude of pride. God judged Lucifer's attitude as *sin* (see Isaiah 14:12-14 and Ezekiel 28:16-17). God hates pride and He will not tolerate it in His presence. Pride is at the root of jealousy and will manifest in wrong and hurtful behaviour towards others.

In Diotrephes' case, he used malicious words against John. The word *malicious* is defined as *"characterized by malice; intending or intended to do harm."*[23] The word *malice* is also defined as *"the desire to harm someone; ill will"*[24]. This is serious! This kind of behaviour brings much hindrance to the work of the Gospel. In 3 John 1:11 we are told not to imitate this kind of behaviour. In his earlier letter (1 John 4:19-21), John exhorts us that we cannot say that we love God if we hate our brother. In fact, he states that person who hates his brother is a liar when he claims that he loves God. The reason he is considered a liar is because of the fact that God's love ought to change our hearts and cause us to have love for other believers in Christ.

My brothers and sisters in Christ, we need to deal with every trace of hatred, jealousy and competition and get it out of our hearts! We must not allow hatred, jealousy or feel hurt when others are sent in by God to minister in our area. We are all workers in His vineyard, there is a harvest to be won, all hands are needed and God is not hindered by the color of our skin, our gender, age, and/or status. Perhaps this is why Jesus did not make such distinctions in the great commission when He said, "*...go ye into all the world and preach the gospel to every creature.*" (Mark 16:15)

It is also important to mention Paul's instructions to the Thessalonian believers, "*...get to know those who labour among you...*" (1 Thessalonians 5:12, Amp). The importance of this is to know *the character* as well as *the integrity* of those who labour among us in the work of the Gospel. This is what we see John the apostle doing in his letter to Gaius as he speaks of both Diotrephes and Demetrius in light of their conduct. He points out the traits of them both indicating that he knew them by personal encounter and experience of them. His knowledge of them was not from a place of mere gossip. Therefore, when considering other workers in the Kingdom, we must keep in mind this important aspect in ministry and that is, we must know them. This to me speaks of relationship and accountability. We need each other. We also need people to be able to speak into our lives in order that we will be truly effective in our areas of ministry.

As reported by John the apostle, John commends Gaius for the way he received the fellow workers in the gospel. He was hospitable to them, and it was also reported how they were welcomed by him:

> *Beloved, you do faithfully whatever you do for the brethren and for strangers, who have borne witness of your love before the church. If you send them forward on their journey in a manner worthy of God,*

*you will do well, because they went forth **for His name's sake**, taking nothing from the Gentiles. We therefore ought to receive such, that we may become fellow workers **for the truth*** (3 John 1:5-8, NKJV, emphasis mine).

We are fellow workers *for His name's sake* and *for the truth*. We must not lose sight of the goal of the Gospel. It is not so that we can promote ourselves or lift up some ministry name. We are called to simply to declare the good news of the Gospel of Jesus Christ - to make Him known and to make Him famous. John the apostle makes mention of Demetrius in light of his good example:

Demetrius hath good report of all men, and of the truth itself: yea, and we also bear record; and ye know that our record is true (3 John 1:12).

Did you see that? Demetrius had a good report! His reputation was so clear that not only his friends could recommend him but the apostles as well. What was it that made him reputable? It was that he held to the truth. Those that hold to the truth of the Gospel are those who will not have behaviour like that of Diotrephes – wanting to have the preeminence or speaking malicious words against others. Instead of being a hindrance to the work of the Gospel and to those God sends, they are non-discriminative and are a blessing wherever they go. They manifest Christ-like behaviour and have genuine love for all of God's people.

After thoroughly searching for several years, I have come to find from the Word of God that nowhere in scripture do we have more authority in our place of birth than those who are from somewhere else. Our authority comes from obeying Jesus, *"All authority is given unto me (Jesus)... go ye therefore..."*[25]. Also we do not have the right to oppose fellow workers in the Gospel who are from other places. That kind of teaching is in fact, *discrimination*. The definition for the word *discriminate* means to *make an unjust or prejudicial distinction in the treatment of different categories of people, especially on the grounds of race, sex or age.*[26] That is a work of Satan. It is not the heart of Jesus for all mankind. My hearts cry is to see all of God's people go forth and work towards the return of Jesus with nothing holding them back.

However, once we know the truth of His Word we can have confidence in His truth. Once we understand *where* our spiritual authority is based, we will go forward with boldness and trust in the Lord. Once we realize who we are *in Christ*, we will accomplish great things in His Name as we learn to seek His face and be led by His Spirit as Romans 8:14 states, *"for as many as are led by the Spirit of God, these are the sons of God"* (NKJV).

The Word *led* in this passage of scripture is the Greek word *ag'-o* - "A primary verb; properly *to lead*; by implication *to bring, drive,* (reflexively) *go,* (specifically) *pass* (time), or (figuratively) *induce.*[27] God wants to lead and to bring us into the destiny He has called each of us into. He wants to be in the *driver* seat. He will show us where to go. He will cause His plans to come to pass. He will *induce* us with His power to enable us to bring forth His plans and purposes in the places He has called each one of us to go to.

The word *sons* speaks of a maturity, as well as our place of privilege in the family of God, which means our spiritual privilege. It is upon being born again, that we are in the family of God. This privilege is from the position of being in Christ, where we are seated in *"heavenly places"* (see Ephesians 2:6). Heavenly is not earthly. It is in the spiritual realm of the Kingdom of God; not depending upon our status in this world.

THE ULTIMATE MOTIVATION

Jesus lived and expressed the very heart of God. As quoted before in this book and so often in many other places around the globe, John 3:16 shows us why God sent His Son: *"For God so loved..."* *He so loved*. Love was His ultimate motivation. This was not just a feeling or an emotion but an action word. We must have a fresh revelation of His love for us and for every human being ever created in this world. Jesus went all the way to the cross because He loved you and me. The apostle John writes these words:

> *Beloved, let us love one another, for love is God and everyone who loves is born of God and knows God. He who does not love does not know God, for God is love. In this the love of God was manifested to-*

ward us, that God sent His only begotten Son into the world, that we might live through Him. In this is love, not that we loved God, but that He loved us and sent His Son to be the propitiation for our sins. Beloved, if God so loved us, we also ought to love one another... There is no fear in love; but perfect love casts out fear, because fear involves torment. But he who fears has not been made perfect in love. We love Him because He first loved us... And this commandment we have from Him: that he who loves God must love his brother also
(1 John 4:7-11, 18-19, 21, NKJV).

Paul reminds us in his letter to the Corinthians believers that if we do not have love then all that we do is nothing (see 1 Corinthians 13:1-3). This is still true for us as believers today. Love is the number one rule. Paul challenges us regarding our motivation for going forth in His Name and that our ministering the Gospel of Jesus Christ ought to be that the Love of God compels us to go. When we are influenced by His love, we will not get caught in the trap of discrimination or self-righteousness or pride. Instead, our main goal will be to please our Lord and reach the lost because that is why Jesus came. Are you glad that you have heard the good news and are now a born again child of God? Was is not shared with you in order that you too would be saved? Let us never forget where God has brought us from.

Conclusion

For the love of Christ compels us, because we judge thus: that if One died for all, then all died; and He died for all, that those who live should live no longer for themselves, but Him who died for them and rose again.
(2 Corinthians 5:14-15, NKJV)

We need to understand that as new creations in Christ, this life we now live is no longer about us. Our identity is found in who we are in Christ. It is about the Lord and what He desires in this life. His heart is for the lost. He wants the lost to be reached at any cost. We must catch His heart.

Jesus said, *"Come to me, all you who labour and are heavy laden, and I will give you rest. Take my yoke upon you and learn from me, for I am gentle and lowly in heart, and you will find rest for your souls. For my yoke is easy and My burden is light"* (Matthew 11:28-30, NKJV). Let us learn from the life of Jesus. As a human being who was tempted on all counts even as we are, yet did not sin (see Hebrews 4:15), Jesus walked in His identity as the Son of God and in Divine Authority. He was motivated by the love of the Father. The battle for kingdom identity has been won. We are children of the most High God, led by His Spirit, rooted in His love, complete in Him. Let us walk in it together and see mighty victories for the kingdom of God as the end time harvest of the earth comes in.

Let us all work towards the return of Jesus!

END NOTES

1. Canada's First Nations - Native Civilisations copyright 2000 The Applied History Research Group www.ucalgary.ca/applie_history/tutot/firstnations/civilisations.html

2. ibid

3. *Hathaway, Warren E., Discipleship Bible School session 2014, NTOMI (Ft. Providence, NT)*

4. Genesis 1:26-27

5. Genesis 3:1-24, Romans 5:12-14

6. John R. Cross, *The Stranger on the road to Emmaus*, 3rd ed. (Olds, AB: Good Seed International copyright, 1997, 1998, 1999, 2000, 2001, 2002, 2003, 2004), pg 264

7. Hebrew # 87, Strong's Exhaustive Concordance: Strong's Exhaustive Concordance of the Bible by James Strong – Hendrickson Publishers, P.O. Box 3473 Peabody, MA 01961-3473

8. Hebrew # 85, Strong's Exhaustive Concordance: Strong's Exhaustive Concordance of the Bible by James Strong – Hendrickson Publishers, P.O. Box 3473 Peabody, MA 01961-3473

9. Hebrew # 3290, Strong's Exhaustive Concordance: Strong's Exhaustive Concordance of the Bible by James Strong – Hendrickson Publishers, P.O. Box 3473 Peabody, MA 01961-3473

10. *BDB Dictionary "Israel"*, MySword for Android version 5.4, Copyright ©2011-2014 by Riversoft Ministry

11 *Thayer Definition "Saul"*, MySword for Android version 5.4, Copyright ©2011-2014 by Riversoft Ministry

12 *Thayer Definition "Paul", MySword for Android version 5.4, Copyright ©2011-2014 by Riversoft Ministry*

13 Hebrew # 4138, Strong's Exhaustive Concordance: Strong's Exhaustive Concordance of the Bible by James Strong – Hendrickson Publishers, P.O. Box 3473 Peabody, MA 01961-3473

14 Oxford Dictionary of English: Oxford University Press Great Clarendon Street, Oxford 0X2 6DP, Third Edition 2010, ©1998, 2003, 2005, 2010, pg. 991

15 Greek # 3504, Strong's Exhaustive Concordance: Strong's Exhaustive Concordance of the Bible by James Strong – Hendrickson Publishers, P.O. Box 3473 Peabody, MA 01961-3473

16 Greek # 5485, Strong's Exhaustive Concordance: Strong's Exhaustive Concordance of the Bible by James Strong – Hendrickson Publishers, P.O. Box 3473 Peabody, MA 01961-3473

17 Strong's Exhaustive Concordance: Strong's Exhaustive Concordance of the Bible by James Strong – Hendrickson Publishers, P.O. Box 3473 Peabody, MA 01961-3473

18 Strong's Exhaustive Concordance: Strong's Exhaustive Concordance of the Bible by James Strong – Hendrickson Publishers, P.O. Box 3473 Peabody, MA 01961-3473

19 Greek # 1849, Strong's Exhaustive Concordance: Strong's Exhaustive Concordance of the Bible by

James Strong – Hendrickson Publishers, P.O. Box 3473 Peabody, MA 01961-3473

20 ibid

21 Strong's Exhaustive Concordance: Strong's Exhaustive Concordance of the Bible by James Strong – Hendrickson Publishers, P.O. Box 3473 Peabody, MA 01961-3473

22 Oxford Dictionary of English: Oxford University Press Great Clarendon Street, Oxford 0X2 6DP, Third Edition 2010, ©1998, 2003, 2005, 2010, pg. 1399

23 Oxford Dictionary of English: Oxford University Press Great Clarendon Street, Oxford 0X2 6DP, Third Edition 2010, ©1998, 2003, 2005, 2010, pg. 1071

24 Ibid

25 Matthew 28:18b-19a

26 Oxford Dictionary of English: Oxford University Press Great Clarendon Street, Oxford 0X2 6DP, Third Edition 2010, ©1998, 2003, 2005, 2010, pg. 501

27 Greek # 71, Strong's Exhaustive Concordance: Strong's Exhaustive Concordance of the Bible by James Strong – Hendrickson Publishers, P.O. Box 3473 Peabody, MA 01961-3473

To order more copies of this book, find books by other Canadian authors, or make inquiries about publishing your own book, contact PageMaster at:

PageMaster Publication Services Inc.
11340-120 Street, Edmonton, AB T5G 0W5
books@pagemaster.ca
780-425-9303

catalogue and e-commerce store
www.ShopPageMaster.ca

ABOUT THE AUTHOR:

Rev. Velma D White is a Cree First Nations missionary who currently resides in Ft. Providence, Northwest Territories. She has been ministering mainly among First Nations people with *New Testament Outreach Ministries Int.* since the year 2000. She also teaches at the *NTOMI-Discipleship Bible School* in Ft. Providence and is a worship leader for the ministry. Velma loves Jesus, His people and the lost. She has a passion to see First Nations people everywhere reached with the true message of the Gospel of Jesus Christ. Her desire is to see them come to know who they are in Christ and to be raised up for the work of the ministry.